M000194366

COVID-19 and Humanity's Spiritual Awakening

Forrest Rivers

Also by Forrest Rivers

The Hippie Revival and Collected Writings

This title is available at your local retailer, online retailers, or may be ordered by visiting

https://ConsciousLiving.Media

https://Covid-19Book.info

COVID-19 and Humanity's Spiritual Awakening

Forrest Rivers

Conscious Living Media / Vizia Fiction
Tucson, Arizona
USA

Copyright © 2021 Forrest Rivers

All rights reserved. No part of this publication may be reproduced or transmitted in any form (electronically, photocopying, recording, or otherwise) without the prior written permission of the copyright owner and the publisher of this book.

All rights reserved, including the right to reproduce this material. Re-selling through electronic or retail outlets without permission of the author and publisher is illegal and punishable by law.

This book is not intended to provide emotional, psychological, or financial advice. Readers are encouraged to seek professional counsel on any personal or financial matters.

Cover and Interior design: Aaron C. Yeagle
ISBN: 978-1-7358425-1-6

Printed in the United States of America

Table of Contents

Introduction:

1. Our moment of Awakening
2. Transcending our Fear of Death
3. Seeing Beyond Dualism
4. Radical Love
5. Choose Faith Not Belief
6. Let Go, let God
7. Spiritual Freedom
8. Meditation as a Shield of Light
9. Signs of Hope
10. Dreams worth Chasing
11. Merging into One
12. If the Earth Could Speak
13. Native Wisdom
14. Reviving an Old Vision for a New World
15. Real Democracy
16. A More Fulfilling Economy
17. Back to Religion's Roots
18. The Promise of Self-Sufficiency
19. A Message
20. An Art Renaissance
21. The Spiritual War
22. Shapers of our Destiny
23. One World Healing
24. To Be and To Love

Appendix:

1. Suggested Spiritual Books to Read during Social Distancing
2. Meditations

Introduction

"Light Comes gently, slowly, but surely it comes."

-Swami Vivekananda-

"Hope is important because it can make the present moment less difficult to bear. If we believe that tomorrow will be better, we can bear a hardship today."
— Thich Nhat Hanh-

When the clock struck midnight on January 1st, 2020, marking the start of a new decade, no one could have possibly imagined the utter chaos and unpredictability that would bring in the new year. As everyone well knows, the deadly Coronavirus began its silent march across the world infecting and claiming the lives of countless millions. From the very beginning, it became resoundingly clear that this pandemic would dramatically alter the course of humanity for the foreseeable future. Phrases and practices like "social distancing", "essential and non-essential workers", "flattening the curve", "stay at home orders", the mass wearing of face coverings in public places, and curbside food and retail pickup came to form the COVID-19 consciousness.

The far reach of the virus into every facet of our lives also forced us to confront our deepest existential anxieties and fears. For example, the elderly and those with preexisting health conditions had to quickly come to terms with the fact that they could succumb to the virus at any moment. And millions of workers laid off from their jobs had little choice but to navigate the waters of extreme financial hardship. For medical professionals on the frontlines, death, and dying in the age of COVID has become a tragic yet valuable daily reminder of the impermanent nature of life. Finally, seekers on the path of higher consciousness have found the pandemic to be a wonderful opportunity to work with the immense suffering that the virus has created. In essence, COVID-19 has had the effect of awakening humanity.

When the outbreak began and the college I teach at was ordered to shutdown mid-semester, I recall skeptically thinking, "how bad could this virus really be?" Apparently, much worse than I could have ever imagined at the time. In just the first two months of the outbreak, here, in the United States, hospitalization and fatality rates reached alarming levels, businesses were forced to shut down, and a record number of people filed for unemployment compensation. Meanwhile, shoppers fearing a breakdown in the nation's food supply resorted to panic shopping at grocery and retail stores. The scene of empty shelves and runs on key necessities like toilet paper (I will never completely understand that one!) only added to the fear of the moment. As the virus raged out of control like a wildfire, the economy went into complete free fall as American state governments tightened shutdown orders to suppress the outbreak. Just when it appeared that things could not grow any more chaotic, the murder of George Floyd (an unarmed black man) occurred at the hands of the Minneapolis Police. This horrific event coincided with the peak of the first "surge" of COVID-19 and set off a wave of protests in most major US cities.

Together, these events made for an apocalyptic like setting straight out of Hollywood films. For many, COVID 19 appeared to be a harbinger of mass chaos and unspeakable tragedy. However, if we can still our minds and fully be with the immensity of this moment, we can start to see a different narrative emerging. These profound words from the infinitely wise and late spiritual teacher, Baba Ram Dass, have helped me to reorient my perspective of these unprecedented events:

"Suffering is the sandpaper that awakens people."

Rather than react to the unsettling chain of events surrounding COVID-19 with fear and dread, we each have the choice to embrace it as the "sandpaper" that helps us all awaken and take a faithful leap in our consciousness. Some realized beings might even go as far as to say, that this pandemic appeared in part to awaken us from our collective delirium of mindless conformity and separation. It is this hopeful perspective of COVID-19 that grounds each of the chapters that follow. Contemplative explorations on such enduring themes as our fear of death, faith, the power of meditation practice, destiny, the value of indigenous wisdom, and radical love are each set against the context of this unique moment in history. Each chapter is intended to inspire a new and soulful direction for humanity.

I invite you, the reader and fellow seeker, to join me on this moving path of spirit. These unsettling times can make us feel more divided, alone, and afraid. Or they can empower us to look within and realize our common ties with all of humanity. Never, have we been so united in our mutual experience of suffering. And at no other time have we all been so deeply called upon to transcend all that separates us. The moment of our awakening has arrived, and we have this frightening yet potentially illuminating pandemic to thank for it. Deep in my own soul, I have faith that we can each meet this moment of terrible suffering with loving awareness and evolve into more soulful and compassionate beings. In the end, that is our ultimate destiny.

Forrest Rivers

The Great Smoky Mountains

October 31st, 2020

1. Our Moment of Awakening

Amid all the fearful media coverage and chaos surrounding the COVID-19 pandemic lies a hidden truth that is just now beginning to come into the light: from a spiritual perspective this public health crisis has been something of a collective blessing in disguise. While the world has been hard hit with both existential and economic catastrophes, something altogether beautiful and inspiring bubbled up from beneath the surface. That "something" is unity and compassion. At first glance, it might appear that mounting death tolls (particularly, among the elderly and those with pre-existing conditions) and runaway unemployment defined the narrative of this virus's fallout. However, what has not been adequately accounted for by much of the media is that this ordeal has pulled us all closer together. For the first time since possibly World War II, the whole of humanity has been forced to confront the painful truth that a collective mindset of ignorance, intolerance, hated, and greed only winds up producing negative consequences for us all.

COVID-19 has had the effect of exposing long-standing societal injustices that have left many questioning the values guiding humanity. For example, in countries like America, the crisis has made it crystal-clear that the needs of living and breathing people should come before the pursuit of profit for a wealthy and connected few. Basic social services that most industrialized nations enjoy, like comprehensive paid sick leave and universal health care have long been absent in the United States. This is partly because U.S. society has long prioritized the "bottom line" economic concerns of powerful corporations over the well-being of its own citizens. Gratefully, all of this is starting to change. In the initial months of the outbreak, the number of ordinary Americans and politicians demanding the implementation of both programs soared. It now seems more likely than ever that paid sick leave and universal health care will soon become permanent fixtures of the U.S. system. This is all indicative of a positive move in the direction of a kinder and gentler society.

There is further evidence that our world is growing more compassionate and united in response to the virus. In the earliest days of the pandemic, it was widely reported that many retired doctors and nurses in the United States, Canada, and Europe came out of retirement to courageously serve the sick and dying. Many medical professionals have taken their Hippocratic Oath seriously. Thank you to those brave souls! In several U.S. and Canadian cities, such as Vancouver, B.C., and Portland, Oregon, groups of

private citizens organized to provide desperately
needed health care and shelter to homeless
populations badly impacted by the pandemic.
Companies, like Portland's Jupiter Hotel, even got in
on the act of caring for this highly marginalized and
impacted group by donating several of its rooms to
self-quarantine in. Numerous reports also began to
surface that initial donations to local food banks
soared when the government-mandated shutdowns of
the economy began.

Many Hindus have long believed that the entire
Cosmos moves in a perpetual cycle between dark ages
(those defined by ego, discord, and contention) and
ages of enlightenment in which awareness of our
divine nature prevail. We may be in the opening stages
of a planetary shift in consciousness, from such a dark
age to one of enlightenment. (The Hindus believe we
are still in a dark age that they call the Kali Yuga,
although the approximate start and end date of this
era are debated by Hindu scholars.) If this worldview

is considered, the emergence of COVID-19 has not been some cruel twist of fate or a cosmic 'hiccup,' but is rather something that emerged in this moment of space and time to jolt us out of our heartless egotism. Despite the heavy and tragic loss of life left in its wake, COVID-19 may soon come to be regarded as one of our light posts on the path of humanity's spiritual awakening.

Perhaps, our age of enlightenment is just around the corner. All we have to do is awaken enough to recognize the signs!

II. Transcending Our Fear of Death

A hallmark of any global pandemic is our emphasis on the number of dead and dying. Understandably, the repetition of mounting casualties by the media has provoked deep anxiety and fear among the people. However, if we shift our perspective just a bit, the existential threat that this virus represents provides us all with a wonderful opportunity to confront our fears of death. Why is confronting this intrinsic fear so important? Because it allows us to live our lives with a greater sense of freedom and equanimity. Many seekers of eastern faiths believe that making peace with the inevitability of our death is among the highest spiritual practices we can pursue. When we transcend our own of it, we unlock a gate to live more deeply in the present moment. When we do so, we follow our Dharma, our cosmic destiny, and all of humanity benefits.

COVID-19 has provided all of us with a unique chance to engage in such spirited reflection on our mortality. It has also served as a dramatic reminder that one day, sooner or later, we are all going to die. This pandemic has also taught us that as we draw closer to our death, we are each presented wi paths to follow. We can choose the first and conditioned road of denying the inevitable p our physical bodies and blindly grasp the flee nature of this material world. But this choice wi only wind up creating more needless suffering. Just as the Buddha taught, we cannot hold on to any physical forms including our bodies.

Very fortunately, the presence of COVID-19 has also helped many people realize that there is a second path we can follow. We always have the choice to embrace our death by surrendering to the wondrous passage of form back to the "Formless", the "Void", or the "One". Instead of continually running from death's haunting shadow, we have the power to meet it at its doorstep with our hearts fully open to what IS and will soon become. Rather than lament the existential fact that we have no control over the time and manner of our passing, we can choose to become death's supreme inquisitor and ask it all the questions that we already intuitively know the answers to. Death does not have to be a painful and frightening process. We can use this ultimate of transitions for our healing and personal growth.

COVID-19 has also been a refreshing reminder that there is no better way to overcome our fear of death than by actively preparing for it through formal spiritual practices like work with the dying and meditation. Stephen Levine, a late and influential spiritual teacher spent countless years working with people who were, as many Hindus say, close to "dropping their bodies". His experiences led him to write a profound and groundbreaking book titled, "*A Year to Live: How to Live This Year as if It Were Your Last.*" Drawing from his years of work with the

Living/Dying Project, a non-profit he co-founded that works on creating a loving space for people to die consciously. Levine showed the profound emotional and spiritual benefits of living each day as if it were your last.

Baba Ram Dass, the late pioneer of human consciousness and the author of the seminal classic, *Be Here Now*, was a close friend of Levine's who also spent considerable time co-founding and working with the Living/Dying Project. In many of his books and recorded lectures, Ram Dass credited his many decades of work with the dying as the deepest spiritual work that he ever did on himself. According to this beloved teacher, the more one consciously works with those nearing death the less one comes to fear their own. He was fond of teaching that if you can learn to "keep your heart open in hell," through embracing the painful emotions that watching another dies engenders, then the opportunity to transcend your fears also becomes possible. Once your heart breaks,

9

you can fall back into the wisdom of your deathless self.

In the Theravada Buddhist tradition, monks partake in regular mindfulness meditation exercises on their deaths (this practice is called *Maranasati*). The central aim of these contemplative sessions is to cultivate a deeper awareness and acceptance of death. Eventually, after years of this practice, monks become so comfortable with the absolute and impermanent nature of their physical world that they completely shed their fear of what may be called the "great unspeakable". The result is that they live with a greater sense of joy, fulfillment, and compassion. In the end, learning to live a more joyous, fulfilled, and compassionate life is the goal of all spiritual seeking. COVID-19 has been presented to us as a fierce gift, so that we might get on with the journey of overcoming one of our greatest existential fears.

III. Seeing Beyond Dualism

For a long time now, the world has been sadly divided by such identity markers as politics, religion, social class, geographic location, and race. Liberals vs conservatives, religious fundamentalists vs atheists, rich vs poor, urban dwellers vs rural farmers, and the white race vs just about every other racial minority group. Is it really much of a surprise, then, that this division has spilled over into peoples' reactions to COVID-19? Combine a terrifying public health crisis with a catastrophic economic collapse and the recipe is there for social conflict.

For example, here in the United States, there were two opposing groups of people who quickly emerged in response to the pandemic. On the one "side", were those who felt that the virus represented a grave existential threat. Not surprisingly, these people ascribed to the belief that governments should do everything that was in their power to protect citizens from COVID-19—- even if it meant resigning countless millions to grinding poverty through mandated shutdowns of the economy.

On the other "side", were those who believed that COVID-19 was deliberately overblown by media outlets who had a financial incentive to engineer a climate of fear and serve a political agenda. Individuals with this belief felt that millions of hard-working Americans were recklessly laid off from their jobs and that the shutdowns were a breach of government power and should have been avoided—- even if it came at the cost of hundreds of thousands of deaths among America's most vulnerable populations. Can you see the flaws in both lines of arguments?

In retrospect, the "pro shutdown" groups were indisputably correct for prioritizing the sanctity of human life above all other concerns including the economy. However, the means with which those in power with this belief acted wound up inflicting mass suffering on many through a shocking wave of job layoffs, food insecurity, and long-term financial ruin. In contrast, the "anti-shutdown" folks were absolutely correct in bringing to light the massive economic hardships that befell countless millions of people. However, their perspective can easily be dismissed as incredibly selfish because it sacrifices the priority of saving countless humans' lives for the sake of economic security and profit.

What can possibly be done to ease the division among a people in crisis? Once again, we can turn to the wisdom of the east for answers. Each of the major eastern traditions teach that all pairs of seeming opposites are really connected as one. For example, the day is only the day because there is night. We only recognize wisdom because ignorance exists. And the warmth of summer is only blissfully enjoyed because the cold of winter is faithfully endured. The true and underlying nature of reality lies beyond all dualism.

In Zen Buddhism, when a student comes before a Roshi (a great master), they are given a type of spiritual riddle, or Koan, to solve that is designed to break the mind from its restless stream of dualistic thoughts. In the Upanishads, a collection of mystical Hindu teachings, each passage exalts the seeker who, through years of meditation and the spirit of selfless service, are able to finally see beyond all dualism and experience the boundless essence of Brahman, or God, itself. In the Tao Te Ching, an ancient text of Taoist philosophy, its sage-author, Lao Tzu, even goes as far to say that all seeming polarities give birth to each other:

"When the world knows beauty as beauty,
ugliness arises
When it knows good as good, evil arises
Thus, being and non-being produce each
other
Difficult and easy bring about each other
Long and short reveal each other
High and low support each other
Music and voice harmonize each other
Front and back follow each other."

Seeing the inherent unity within all pairs of seeming

opposites is the key to learning how not to cast

judgment on another person's beliefs or opinions. It is

also the secret, then, in promoting peaceful dialogue

and cohabitation. In today's highly polarized world, is

it truly possible to live in harmony with this valuable

wisdom? I hold out hope that the answer to this

question is yes. Deep down, I genuinely believe that all

people desire to live in peace with all others. It is only

our ignorance (which we all have in something) that

holds us back from becoming one.

Consider these two illustrative examples of our unconscious ignorance:

Many people who were in support of the shutdowns tended to reside in more urban areas, leaned more liberal politically and worked in higher-paying white-collar jobs. Not surprisingly, these groups held more favorable views of the shutdowns. Why? Because due to their denser populations, urban centers suffered from far higher casualties than rural areas. It was also easier and much more practical for urban white-collar workers to transition to remote work. Accordingly, the overall economic impact on this group of highly educated workers was negligible compared to the struggles endured in more blue-collar occupations.

Short of having been raised in a working-class family or living in the countryside, what could a liberal, white-collar urbanite possibly know about the very real economic struggles felt by more conservative rural laborers? From the latter group's point of view, they have watched their multi-generational farms and businesses fail and their livelihoods dissolve in response to a crisis (mostly) taking place far away from home in the cities. Further stoking tensions was the fact that the strictest shutdown measures (see California and Michigan for example) were ordered by other liberal, wealthy governors.

Flipping the script, what could a rural blue-collar worker possibly know about the unimaginable suffering experienced in urban areas like New York City---- where the death toll from COVID-19 was so high that some morgues were unable to store all the bodies? If someone from a rural area visited a major city for even a few days and interviewed family members and hospital workers (like my own sister who is an ER doctor) who watched a loved one or patient die from the virus would they still think that it was "overblown?"

In these troubled times, we must transcend our dualistic way of seeing the world and live with greater wisdom in our day to day lives. This means, that we

17

need to learn how to see the "other perspective," and see that our ways of relating are not that different. If we can broaden our minds and open our hearts, we may find that all our beliefs wind up folding upon each other in the end.... just as Lao Tzu said they would. Regardless of our political opinions on COVID-19, collectively we are all having to cope with its fallout. It seems to me that we have much to find common ground upon. Finding common ground is the easy part. More difficult is choosing to let go of our egoic conditioning that sees things in terms of black and white. Moving beyond dualism, means, we can cultivate compassion and understanding through what is called "radical love".

IV. Radical Love

As the pandemic continued to rage on, it became painfully obvious to many just how fractured our world had become as a result.... particularly in heavy class-divided nations like the United States. There, COVID-19 revealed the shocking and unconscious able disparities that exist between rich and poor. It has also demonstrated that the line between fact and fiction has been badly blurred due to sensationalized and partisan reporting by the media on all sides. The emergence of anti-shutdown protests also showed that Americans couldn't even agree on whether to continue with extreme social distancing measures or to begin re-opening the economy.

Frustratingly, it would appear that politics (the world's current expression of collective ego) has divided us again. However, the negative consequences of separation are being more profoundly felt because of the high stakes of the public health crisis. What is clear is that both anger and frustration have boiled over among large sections of the population. The question now is how can humanity meet this moment in a way that alleviates suffering? The answer is to be found through radical love.

When Jesus was nailed to the cross, he uttered these words: "Father, forgive them, for they do not know what they are doing." Those powerful words were extended as a prayer of forgiveness for his tormenters. They were also an expression of the highest form of radical love. When Gandhi guided his beloved India to independence through leading a perilous 24-day Salt March (which eventually cost him his life) that too, was an example of radical love. The Reverend Martin Luther King Jr. endured beatings, death threats, prison, and eventually his assassination to liberate his nation from the scourge of racial apartheid. He also expressed the beautiful vision of radical love. When Vietnamese monks self-immolated themselves in protest of South Vietnam's persecution of Buddhist monks, that too was an act of radical love. Of course, each of these beings is rightfully remembered for their willingness to surrender their lives in pursuit of noble objectives. Fortunately, one does not need to become a martyr to act in accord with this divine

principle. There are many acts of radical love that we can all engage in at this very moment to relieve suffering and hardship. Some examples include:

- feeding the hungry
- Providing clothing for the poor
- Caring for the sick
- Attending to those who have lost a loved one due to COVID-19

- Uplifting elderly neighbors who may continue to live in extreme conditions of social isolation

It is especially telling that the great Indian Saint, Neem Karoli Baba, taught his devotees that the act of feeding the hungry was such a high expression of radical love that it could be used as a path to one's enlightenment. It would be wise to resist being emotionally pulled into the political drama of our leaders' response to this pandemic. For the sake of humanity, it would be much more constructive for us all to make ourselves instruments of service and lead with our hearts. After all, this is the essence of radical love: treating the suffering of others as if it were your own AND having the courage to relieve another's suffering even if it comes at a great personal cost to you. The courageous display of such a spirit of selflessness is what imbues the expression of love with its truly radical component.

In the end, COVID-19 represents a rare opportunity for us all to undergo a paradigm shift in consciousness from one focused on self-serving ends to one grounded in the spirit of loving-kindness. However, to make this shift, we must first have faith that it is even possible. Faith, not belief, is the golden horse that will lead us into the fertile valley of peace and oneness!

Forrest Rivers

V. Choose Faith Not Belief

Faith is a beautiful thing. It can be compared to a budding flower, intuitively growing into its purpose to inspire and give life. However, this inspiring quality is too often confused with belief. Faith and belief are not the same things. Belief says: through my rational mind I **think** all is one. Faith says: within my soul, I **know** all is one. Belief thinks. Faith knows. Belief is fleeting and can easily be broken at the first sign of personal struggle.

The reason why belief is so fragile is that it is a projection of the ego. One of the defining characteristics of the ego is that it views the world through the lens of separation. And, because it sees

25

itself as separate from the one reality, its thoughts are not truly rooted in anything but its narrow framework of how it "thinks" the world is. This lack of intuitive knowing may also explain why belief often produces intense religious and political dogmas. In the absence of a more intuitive understanding, one has a flickering faith in their own beliefs and sets out to convert others to validate the "truth" for them.

In contrast to belief is faith. Faith is one's conquering of fear through inner surrender. It is born through an intuitive knowing that is strengthened through heartfelt prayer and meditation. Faith finds its expression through all authentic acts of kindness and is also firmly rooted in one's own direct experience. Another aspect of faith is that it conveys an eternal quality of truth that does not need to be spoken to convert believers. With faith, one has no desire to proselytize because what is known can only be accessed within. The desire to inspire others through sharing wisdom and baring one's soul is a hallmark of faith. The desire to control another's thoughts is a hallmark of belief. The former is the source of inspiration for the sincerest artists, counselors, and seekers. The latter is too often the motivation for politicians and religious leaders. Faith heals and unites. Belief injures and divides.

Unfortunately, these exceptional times have been mostly defined by our attachments to extreme belief. For example, amid the devastating backdrop of COVID-19, there has been an alarming number of people (at least in the US) who very strongly believe that it is grossly overblown despite overwhelming scientific evidence proving the contrary. At the start of the pandemic, I used to be counted among those who believed that it was exaggerated. But then I began hearing direct encounters from medical professionals who witnessed first-hand the destructive impact of this virus on patients. Another dangerous manifestation of extreme belief is the view that this pandemic is a conspiracy hatched by a secret cabal of global elites to submit the world's population to the will of ever-tighter government controls. Internet posts on this very topic have rapidly multiplied on the internet. The effects of such extreme beliefs only wind up producing more unwarranted fear, ignorance, and division in society.

Fortunately for humanity, many people of faith are now coming to see this pandemic through a lens of greater awareness. Such an expression of faith embraces COVID-19 and all the challenges it presents as a golden opportunity to move beyond our present state of ego consciousness. This perspective transcends all political, religious, and societal dogmas because it has everything to do with our evolution as one human family

VI. Let Go, Let God

Like many people, when the outbreak of COVID-19 reached North America I found myself glued to my screen following the latest news. The following questions from the media's early coverage soon arose in my mind:

- ➢ Was the severity of this crisis being manufactured by corporate news outlets seeking to turn record profits?

- ➢ Have I already contracted the virus?

- ➢ Will my elderly parents avoid getting sick?

- ➢ Are world leaders doing all they can to protect us from the pandemic?

- ➢ Should we even look to our governments to protect us or would we better off shifting that responsibility to individuals, families, and communities?

➢ How can I help to alleviate suffering for other people during this time?

These questions danced around my head. Consequently, From the second week of March (the start of social distancing) right on through the first week of May, I spent countless hours reading up on COVID-19 to gain a fuller picture of this unprecedented event. After several weeks of suffering near anxiety attacks brought upon by "news binging", I finally realized I had become consumed by the endless emotional train of confusion, fear, and genuine sadness for the fate of humanity. I suspect that many people have also shared this experience along with me.

Every minute that we obsessively spend surfing the web is a minute we waste living HERE NOW. During times like these, it may be more beneficial for us all to focus our awareness on soulfully rich activities that add to our overall sense of well-being. Establishing daily routines built around uplifting practices like meditation, nature walks, and creative expression can go a long way toward cultivating a peace within ourselves that is effortlessly shared with others struggling to cope. My old meditation teacher, Dave Smith, used to have an awesome saying that helped his students let go of their anxiety and fear when facing challenging life events: "This is how it is now." Simple yet profound wisdom. Far from asking us to close our hearts in response to this crisis, Dave's advice invites us to open our hearts through fully surrendering to what is.... even if what we uncover is discomfort. For that emotion shall also pass.

Sitting in front of our computer or phone day by day reading the news will only fill us with greater anxiety and further render us incapable of mindfully responding to the crisis. When I sat down to write this section I suddenly became aware of my hypocrisy on this point. So, I made the conscious choice to begin

31

each morning with a 30-minute meditation rather than pick up my computer and work myself up into a frenzy over the latest COVID news. For me, this was an empowering choice as it showed that I can control my mind (I was seriously beginning to doubt myself!) and find some semblance of inner peace amid an otherwise fearful climate. If I can empower myself, then you can certainly do it too! Maybe, in addition to my beloved teacher's mantra, we can also adopt a well-known second one that is just as relevant to the times that we live in.... "Let Go, Let God". Learning to let go will instantly bring us more balance, clarity, and peace of my mind. It will also allow us to touch a cherished ideal we hold in our hearts: freedom.

VII. Spiritual Freedom

As much of the world withdrew from public life during the period of stay-at-home orders, it had the effect of making many people reflect on the meaning of freedom in the age of COVID. Through this time of quarantining and social distancing freedom came to mean many different things to people.

For the mostly conservative anti-shutdown protesters in the United States (and to a much lesser extent in Western Europe) freedom came to mean the right to work and operate one's own business without undue interference by the government. For these protesters, it also implied the right to make one's personal decisions as it related to public health. Yet, for other folks, freedom came to mean something different. For many liberal urbanites and senior citizens, freedom came to be seen as the right to be protected from the threats posed by others' irresponsible decisions. In the context of this pandemic, some shoppers' insistence on not wearing face coverings in crowded public places was a dramatic example of such a threat.

Medical workers who have been on the frontline of fighting the virus also arrived at their unique understanding of freedom. My sister, the ER doctor, has expressed to me that she and other medical workers would just like the freedom to be able to perform their (very vital) jobs without meeting significant roadblocks along the way. A prime example of such a roadblock was the US Government's early and colossal failure to provide an adequate number of personal protective equipment (PPE) and testing kits for hospitals.

Most profoundly, a growing number of spiritual seekers have also come to their own unique and personal conceptions of freedom. Many on the path have come to regard freedom as something that extends beyond the individual to one's own conscious choice to use their free will to alleviate suffering. This understanding of freedom is akin, in a Christian sense, to being our brother's keeper. In a Buddhist sense, it is rising to the level of becoming a bodhisattva.... A realized being who reincarnates once more to alleviate suffering. This perspective of freedom has everything to do with the right intentions and challenges everyone to step outside themselves and flow with the great river of life. In the end, the direct acknowledgment of the interrelation of all things is the greatest truth that mystics from all faiths have discovered. Thankfully, it appears that in these times more people are beginning to comprehend that true freedom springs from an awareness that we are all connected. Indeed, we all have the power to shift our perspectives of freedom from what is good for me to what is also good for all of us.

VIII. Meditation as Our Shield of Light

The anxiety that people (particularly the elderly
and those with compromised immune systems) are
feeling is understandable. As is the anxiety that many
millions more have experienced as a result of losing
their jobs amid a pandemic. But what if our anxiety
can be channeled to promote lasting and meaningful
spiritual growth? Enter the practice of meditation. The
extreme existential fear that we are now facing may
inevitably lead many people to turn inwards for some
semblance of peace amid the onslaught of panic and
fear. These times are ripe for all of us to establish a
daily meditation practice through stilling our minds,
opening our hearts, and surrendering to the present

37

moment. The unique conditions of social distancing coupled with our unprecedented access to online mindfulness tools lends itself to the emergence of a 'meditation evolution' among the world's population. A profound and inspiring movement toward higher consciousness could be one remarkable outcome of these trying times. And meditation could be the tool that allows many seekers to tune their dials to the channels of planetary awareness.

Two of the primary purposes of meditation is to learn to let go and to recognize one's relationship with all things. During this period of mass sickness and poverty, metta practice is a great meditation exercise that at once achieves both goals. Metta roughly translates to "benevolence" or "Loving Kindness" in Pali and comes to us from the Buddhist tradition. The purpose of this practice is to focus on cultivating and sending feelings of goodwill to all sentient beings. I was first introduced to this practice in my first group meditation I ever attended. The session was led by

Dave Smith (the meditation teacher from earlier) a highly trained teacher in the Theravadin tradition. Smith, who has made it his life's work to aid in the recovery of those suffering from substance abuse, led us through a 20-minute metta practice. In that first sitting, we were asked to imagine sending rays of love from our hearts to all of humanity. This guided meditation so moved my spirit and opened my being that I began attending Dave's Sunday evening session each week.

Looking back now on that fateful day in early 2013, I am amazed at how completely this simple, yet meaningful practice touched my soul. After seven years of reflection on the power of the practice, I have come to realize why it is so impactful: loving-kindness meditations simultaneously quiet our restless minds and open our wayward hearts. In these uncertain times, what could be more inspiring than sending our deepest wishes of love and goodwill to the planet when we wake up each morning and go to bed each night?

Through the ages, it has been said by more than a few sages that meditation is the highest form of prayer because it breaks down the separation between the external world and our vast inner world. If it feels right for you, you might find the following COVID-19 adapted metta practice helpful:

"Find a comfortable position either sitting cross-legged or on the floor or seated upright on a chair of your choosing. Then, slowly close your eyes and bring your awareness to the center of your heart as you begin to inhale and exhale long deep breaths. As you deeply breathe in and out, imagine filling your heart with a pink or green light (colors of love) on the in breath, and then imagine sending that same light out to the world from your heart on the out-breath as you repeat these words to yourself: may all beings be free, may all beings find peace and may all beings be blessed with good health." Try this practice for 15-20 minutes. But feel free to do this exercise for shorter or longer intervals than what I suggest if it feels more comfortable for you".

Meditation has the power to quiet our minds and open our hearts. Remarkably, too, it could also heal the whole world in a time when we are in desperate need of healing. Two very credible studies on the power of meditation were conducted in Jerusalem and in Lebanon in the 1980s. In both studies, Scientific researchers found convincing evidence of a direct link between the practice of mass metta (loving kindness) circles and lower incidences of war. As originally reported and published in the academic journal of Conflict Resolution (1988), during days of high attendance at a peace meditation held in Jerusalem war deaths in neighboring Lebanon decreased by 76 percent. On those days of intention filled metta practice, crime and traffic tickets in the near vicinity decreased as well. Incredibly, the same study was conducted again (with even stricter controls) and produced the same results as reported in the academic journal of Social Behavior and Personality (2005).

If metta practice can bring peace to a war-torn people imagine what it could accomplish in alleviating all suffering related to COVID-19! When love meets prayer full intentions the possibilities for the evolution of human consciousness are boundless. But how can one go about starting a meditation or prayer circle during periods that require social distancing? Max Reif, a fantastic writer for the conscious writing collective, the Mindfulword.org, may have the answer. In one of his many thoughtful articles written during the shutdowns, Reif relates how he learned to tap into virtual online spiritual communities through Zoom (the interactive web interface program that has soared in popularity during the crisis) to cultivate feelings of loving-kindness:

In Reif's Words:

"I rise, as often as possible, at 5 a.m. At 6:30, I attend "Virtual Morning Arti," an international Zoom gathering of Meher Baba devotees. We recite prayers, sing two spiritual anthems, and then spend an hour sharing whatever songs, poems, messages, or anecdotes people are inspired to contribute. This event often leads me to great heights of joy! While the external world continues its hard slog, my internal world is brought to a point of *shining*—more than before the pandemic I think."

Maybe, we can all follow Reif's example in spreading the seeds of loving-kindness. Is it really a stretch for our imaginations to envision meditation circles popping up all over the world through virtual connections? I do not think so. Besides spreading some much-needed peace and love right now the emergence of such gatherings (even if they are only virtual) will also inspire hope.... the true motor of our human condition.

Forrest Rivers

IX. Signs of Hope

In the earliest days of the pandemic, I recall experiencing a string of negative emotions that have surely been shared by many people around the globe. When the shutdowns began in the United States, my initial feelings were those of anxiety, fear, and paranoia. However, the emotion that really took me for a ride was that of doubt. I have always been a glass "half-full" kind of person. I think I got that quality from my parents who have always taught me to have gratitude and consider how fortunate my circumstances are in comparison to those less well off. So, when I started feeling waves of pessimism overtake me I was both somewhat alarmed and surprised. I thought the following to myself: "how can I possibly expect to uplift others through my words when I can't even uplift myself in a time of great difficulty". After all, I thought, the Reverend Martin Luther King Jr did once famously proclaim the following:

> "The ultimate measure of a man is not where he stands in moments of comfort and convenience, but where he stands at times of challenge and controversy."

In my own mind, I interpreted my feelings of doubt as somehow not "measuring up". After investigating these emotions, I penned the following ballad that was admittedly aimed at uplifting myself as much as others in my orbit:

"A Ballad of Hope Amid a Time of Crisis"

The year was 2020
The world was plagued by a pandemic
that inflicted mass casualties across the land
Countless millions watched in horror

As loved ones fell victim to the virus

Many more struggled to find work and food

As the world's economy

Suffered a catastrophic collapse....

Meanwhile, corrupt and greedy politicians

Stood callously by

As the number of homeless multiplied and starved
around them

With little assistance coming from their maniacal
rulers

Some people resorted to looting and organized crime

To meet their basic needs....

But set against this backdrop of death, fear and
deprivation

A movement of higher consciousness was well
underway

Driven into isolation to control the deadly virus

Citizens of the world came to have gratitude

For all the little things they had taken for granted:

Smiles from passing strangers

Sentimental hugs

Uplifting time spent with dear friends and family

And the sweet joys of live song and dance

Were all things sorely missed and remembered

Nostalgically....

Such expressions of gratitude

So intrinsic to what it means to being human

Triggered cosmic waves

Of beautiful but unintended consequences

For humanity's awakening amid this age of crisis....

Sequestered in their homes for months at end

Some discovered a love for art and creativity

While others found God in books and through online
talks

From enlightened masters....

Souls fortunate enough to have nature out their front
door

Planted a garden or communed with the Earth

Through walking, swimming and biking

Inner reflection became a powerful tool

to confront despair for many more

And the practice of meditation underwent a
resurgence

As did faithful prayer and mindful attention

To each passing moment....

The spirit of selfless service

That was heartlessly neglected by society for far too
long

Began bubbling within the hearts of each man,
woman and child

once more....

FINALLY,

The day came

When it was safe for all to emerge from their houses

But when they re-entered the storm of form

What they found was not the same world as before....

A revolution of the heart had been born

And seeds planted

As all showed a genuine love for one another

And displayed reverence for the Earth

Consuming less and communing with Her more

Everywhere,

The Renaissance in art was felt

As Creative expression flourished

Like rivers flowing into the infinite blue ocean....

For the first time in decades

Young people everywhere

Chose to find meaningful work

Rather than chase the almighty dollar....

Of course,

Many day-to-day things remained the same

Grocery stores were still frequented

Children attended schools

And people still drove long distances

To see kindred spirits in kind

But inwardly,

Humanity had awakened from its stupor

Of vanity, greed and self-absorption....

Upon entering this new world

Every step felt lighter

And the sun seemed to shine

With a greater luminosity

To herald the coming

Of mankind's arrival

And to celebrate

Its most profound realization yet:

All things in life are ONE

And filled with the eternal bliss of the Universe

The age of crisis had given way

To humanity's enlightenment

And the old adage that darkness gives way to light

Assumed a new and precious meaning

In this sacred season of spiritual revival.

Very few words have the potential to move the human soul quite like hope. Hope is to have an unyielding optimism for the future. It is also to have an unshakable faith that all things in this universe unfold lawfully and in harmony with the greater flow. Everything that happens in our lives has a deeper meaning and purpose. The good and bad, the joys and heartaches, as well as uplifting moments and collective tragedies are all equal part reflections of the One. It can feel downright impossible to accept the fact that difficult life events, like the death of loved ones, are as much a part of the cosmic way of things as the birth of a newborn or the discovery of true love. Making peace with suffering can be so challenging that the Buddha, a fully enlightened being, centered his teachings on this very subject. We don't have to like suffering or invite it into our lives. However, if we don't learn to make peace with it we will become lost in it and our hearts will never know the light of hope.

In the context of COVID-19, it is most unfortunate that so many people have lost hope. Many have met the escalating death toll from the pandemic, the ensuing meltdown of the global economy, as well as the shocking levels of political polarization throughout the world with tremendous fear and trepidation. Sadly, this lack of hope can quickly spiral into overwhelming feelings of despair if we are not careful. Runaway drug addiction, spikes in the number of suicides, violent crime, and psychotic breaks are the inevitable side effects of a pessimistic people. Looking at the current state of the world, it is not very difficult to see why many are feeling hopeless at this moment in time. In response to the outbreak, our leaders have badly failed us by putting the needs of their own egos and that illusionary thing we call the "economy", over the health and well-being of the very people they should be serving.

At the same time, a dark cloud of hopelessness has fallen over the countless millions of workers who have permanently lost their jobs to no fault of their own. Indeed, these workers have every reason to feel jaded as they and their loved ones now struggle to make ends meet while their leaders continue living in luxury. But all hope is not lost. COVID-19 has graced us with a fortunate opportunity to hit the reset button and ride a new wave of hope. When people are forced to cope with multiple crises it can have the effect of empowering us to take back control of our lives. Remember, out of darkness comes the light. The calm follows after a storm. The dreary and frigid days of winter give way to the warm and vibrant days of spring's rebirth.

In these uncertain times, hope is our gateway to a more conscious and evolved humanity. It is also our gateway to finding gratitude. Thanks to the world-wide shutdowns the earth had the opportunity to heal, more people are rediscovering their innate connection to nature, families are spending more time together, artists are finding more time to create, and we are all gaining a deeper appreciation for the truly important things in life through this shared experience. Who could argue that a healing earth, deeper communion with nature, more attention to family, a renaissance of art, and a renewed focus on inner development will not bring us closer to the living spirit? Hope is hard wired into our souls. Even if we don't quite have the faith yet to believe it, trust me, hope is ingrained within all of us. In the end, a renewed hope for the fate of humanity may be the single greatest thing that emerges from the storm of COVID-19. That....and the courage to finally chase our dreams.

X. Dreams Worth Chasing

At the height of the government shutdowns, John, a friend of mine from Colorado, shared his dreams with me on a socially distanced and gorgeous hike through the mountains together. In the year leading up to the pandemic, this incredibly talented sound engineer and music booker spent around 80 hours a week working at a music venue. While he found his work satisfying, he confided in me that the long hours and breakneck pace of booking bands six nights a week and running sound for those same acts had taken a toll on him emotionally.

Like many skilled workers in the entertainment industry, John suddenly found himself unemployed when all bars and music venues were forced to shut down as COVID-19 began its reign of terror through the United States. But he was one of the lucky ones. In contrast to the countless millions of frustrated and desperate laid-off workers that would follow, John experienced a smooth transition to the unemployment rolls. He related to me that the time away from his job has provided him with a greater sense of balance and fulfillment in his own life. It has also strengthened his relationship with his wife. Most of all, John's hiatus away from the daily grind has given him the courage to chase his dreams and live his life to the fullest. In July 2020, John and his wife followed their dream to live in an RV and moved off to a remote and beautiful tract of land outside of Moab, Utah.

During this period, stories like John's are growing in number. With ample opportunity to spend contemplating our lives, more people are realizing that now is the perfect time to finally chase their dreams. With death staring us all in the face and with the highest percentage of people out of work since the Great Depression, this moment has carved out an existential crossroads that we are all being called to navigate. Some of the questions we may be asking ourselves now are as follows:

➤ Once this crisis ends, do I want to rejoin the "rat race" once more?

➤ How might following a different path enrich me spiritually?

➤ Is it really too late to change directions and follow my dreams?

➤ How can I best contribute to uplifting the human race?

As more of us begin asking these questions, we will inevitably come to find our answers through moments of spirited self-reflection. In these precious instances, the answers we seek will become clear as day like it has for my friend John. Despite the immense tragedy left in its wake, COVID-19 has been something of a blessing for many who have felt "trapped" in the societal machine for far too long. The conditions are perfect to pour one's time and energy into pursuits that more meaningfully serve the higher qualities of the human spirit.

For other people, like my soul brother Alex, this pandemic and the ensuing economic collapse has only confirmed that he wants to take decisive steps in the next year to leave his job and follow a dream of co-founding an off the grid conscious community with other like-minded beings. In his mind, the economic system has badly failed far too many people and he would like the opportunity to show that a better way is possible. A beautiful and noble dream indeed! So beautiful and noble that I hope to co-found this very community with him!

It is fully within our power to shift the narrative of COVID-19 from one of fear and hopelessness to that of seeing this moment as a rare opportunity to follow our dreams through the grace of suffering. If we can manage to flip the dial of our awareness from pessimism to hope, there is no limit to how far we can go in merging with the One that has been called by many names.

Forrest Rivers

XI. Merging into One

Though I never met him in person, Ram Dass has been among my greatest teachers. Unlike many self-described "gurus", he truly "walked the walk". Without the slightest hint of arrogance or of putting on a show, his life was a genuine reflection of all the themes he lectured and wrote about: love, compassion, humility, peace, suffering, the pitfalls on the spiritual path, and Karma Yoga(the spirit of selfless service). The following is one of my favorite Ram Dass quotes:

> "As we grow in our consciousness, there will be more compassion and more love, and then the barriers between people, between religions, between nations will begin to fall. Yes, we have to beat down the separateness."

In the earliest days of the COVID-19 outbreak, it appeared that Ram Dass's words may have been coming to fruition. The war between nations seemed to no longer matter anymore as the virus, itself, became the common enemy of mankind. For a hopeful moment, it appeared like division along the lines of sex, class, race, religion, and politics would dissolve overnight as the pandemic did not discriminate in choosing its victims. For the first time in our lives, the attainment of a higher collective consciousness was a real possibility. Of course, one of the chief aims of all spiritual traditions is to directly experience this innate connection that all beings share. Call this mystical lifeforce energy that connects all things God. Call it the TAO. Call it the One. Or call it the Great Mystery. In the end, whatever name you call IT by doesn't matter. What matters is the knowledge that such a state of being is possible for humanity to achieve. The early days of the pandemic brought us infinitely closer to recognizing this inspiring state of oneness.

Everywhere, people met this crisis with universal compassion. The ranks of volunteers grew to serve at food banks, younger people came to the aid of their elderly neighbors, groups organized to provide shelter to the homeless, and many began honoring over-looked "essential workers" like grocery store clerks and food delivery drivers. However, as the period of social distancing wore on, the world gradually fell back into its old, programmed patterns of fear and separation along lines of associations.... especially in America. Barely five months into the pandemic the following events took place there: armed protests against the shutdowns, massive street demonstrations in response to the police killing of an unarmed black man in Minneapolis, Minnesota, deepening political polarization, and police/military style rule on the streets.

How could the realization of world peace feel so close yet also so far away? After all, for many people, COVID-19 was perceived as a watershed event that revealed mankind's potential to transcend the illusion of separateness. But as they say, old habits die hard. The peace that we all know is possible still remains unfulfilled. However, rest assured that this pandemic has already had the effect of helping us grow in our consciousness.... just as Ram Dass said. Just weeks before the outbreak of the virus, little on the surface appeared to unite us. But following its emergence, more people are starting to see our common humanity.

No matter the scale of our differences on the surface, we have all gone through this period of hardship and suffering together. Because of that we will also grow stronger together. In this moment, most of us know someone who has been severely impacted by this crisis. Some of us have a friend or loved one who has fallen ill or even died from the virus. Others know someone who has lost their job during the pandemic. Whether we want to admit it or not, all the attention given to our supposed divisions are deliberately intended to stoke fear of one another. Why do the powers that be want to promote such division? So, we turn a blind eye to the profoundly serious abuses of power and lack of inhumanity that are taking place right before our very eyes. If we can quiet our minds and go beyond the egoic mindset of our own leaders, we will see that we are not all that different anyway.

Such demarcations like the color of our skin, the region of the world we happened to be born in, and the religious traditions we have been exposed to are all out of our control. They were left up to fate. When we meet a cat or dog do we discriminate against it based on the color of its fur? Do we decide whether to pet it or not based on the location where it was born and in what manner it connects to the living spirit? Of course, we do not. So, why do we do this with humans? In the end, it should be our greatest hope that this shared experience of suffering will allow us to

see past all the divisions and acknowledge the

inherent soul connection we have as beings of loving

awareness. In the end, we are nothing but loving

awareness.

XII. If the Earth Could Speak

If she could speak, I often wonder what the Earth would say to us at this crucial moment of human suffering? What would she tell us? Would she admonish us for our way of living? Would she encourage us to use COVID-19 for our own awakening? Below, is my probably feeble attempt to give expression to the Earth's wisdom at this truly unprecedented time for humanity.

"A Letter from Earth to Humanity"

Dear Humanity,

Earth here. Remember me? This is your eternal mother who feeds you, quenches your thirst, and gives you this gift of life. It has been a long while since I last wrote to you, but I feel obliged to share my thoughts amid the serious health crisis you currently face.

First, let me say that I'm truly sorry for the heavy loss of life that you've endured. I didn't intend for this virus to have such a devastating impact on you. Please trust that I never act with malicious intent. Always, my acts arise from the perfect harmony of the Cosmos. However, I must confess that I did intend to slow down the engines of the money economy that many among you seem to worship as if it were God itself. More specifically, I aimed to get your kind to reflect on the immense harm you have caused to me and by extension to yourselves.

Sadly, your megalomaniac rulers are mostly to blame for these tragic deaths. In truth, if your systems of power had only cared about the poor, elderly, and most vulnerable in society, many more lives could've been saved. However, your authorities insist on prioritizing this illusionary thing you call money over the well-being of all of Earth's inhabitants. Greed and a lack of reverence for life is a creed that only results in mass suffering. The great prophets of all your religious traditions taught as much. This all brings me to my main point for writing you this letter: to inspire reflection. I hope this pandemic has brought your species to these three revelations....

First revelation: You're at my mercy

I hope the past months have served to awaken you to the fact that you're at my mercy. Through this virus, I've clearly shown you that I can quickly summon the forces of nature and easily topple your structures of hubris! And.... I've always been able to do so by producing natural disasters like pandemics, tornadoes, hurricanes, earthquakes, tsunamis, floods, and volcanic eruptions.

Please know that I give you everything you need to thrive and flourish: plentiful food and water, rarefied air to fill your lungs with, majestic mountains to climb and gain perspective upon, crystal-clear lakes and rivers to bathe and cool off in, beautiful animals to bond with, and sacred plants to heal and enlighten you. In short, your species is just one tiny fragment of my infinite consciousness. Without me, there is no you. We're not separate, but one.

Please also know that when you build structures that wind up harming me, you're only harming yourself. It's my *dharma*, my divine duty, to protect all that is holy. So, when your species harms my being, I'm obligated to destroy those very structures.

Second revelation: Your way of life is destructive

This unfolding pandemic has painfully revealed how unwisely your species has been living. A truly civilized people teach and live by the values of peace, unity, and love. A truly civilized people also realize their inherent unity with the Earth and would never do me harm. A truly civilized people are those who cultivate the presence of love and kindness within their culture. Based on your current actions, it appears that your political leaders and captains of industry show little care for the fate of our planet. Massive deforestation, catastrophic climate-change-related events, oil and nuclear spills, the widespread contamination of rivers, lakes, and oceans, as well as the mass extinction of many species are just a sample of how your worship of consumerism has desecrated my body and spirit.

I hope this pandemic has provided a moment of valuable introspection for you. For in the wake of the shutdown of your industries, I actually began to heal. Did you know that for a brief period when the shutdowns began, many gathered in India's urban centers and could see my glorious snowcapped peaks for the first time in over half a century?!?! I can't begin to describe how great it felt to have this respite from your rampant development schemes! My children, it felt so nice to breathe again!

Third revelation: Look to Indigenous Traditions to Guide You

Despite the misguided ways of your dominant culture, there is a path to follow that will bring you eternal peace, harmony, and union with me. The sacred and time-honored traditions of your indigenous peoples hold the secrets to both your future happiness and survival. No matter where or when my beloved guardians have emerged, they've all shared these three things in common beyond space and time:

- A deep and lived inborn belief that the Earth is sacred and is the supreme source of all revelatory wisdom
- Established lifestyles in which humans take only the bare minimum of resources they need from me to survive
- A long and hallowed commitment to defend me from the onslaughts of society's plunderers

Sadly, you find yourself at a very perilous crossroads. At this moment, you so desperately NEED the wisdom of your indigenous peoples, but you've destroyed the very foundations of their cultures. Rather than honor these faithful devotees of the Earth, you insist on desecrating their sacred lands and converting them to your diabolical industrial creed. Can't you see that you have relegated these proud cultures to a life of deprivation and detachment from their spiritual traditions?

Shame on all your "leaders" for their rapacious arrogance and lack of compassion. And shame on you, the people, for your willing complacency and lack of courage to stand up for what is right! Amid this health crisis, have many of you even stopped to consider how badly this pandemic may be hurting your indigenous communities... those very same communities that have been made vulnerable by your culture's ruthless predations over the centuries? Amid this crisis, you've shown some concern for your elderly and those with underlying health conditions. However, have you extended much direct aid to sick native elders who

73

hold the ancient knowledge of YOUR survival through their declining languages and traditions?

I wish to end this letter with a positive and uplifting message. It's never too late to change your ways. If humanity decides to heed these three revelations that I have laid out before you, then the balance of the Earth can be restored and my dream of an everlasting union with you can be realized. Know that I'm pulling for you to succeed. For if you succeed, we both succeed. The choice is yours. Use your gift of free will wisely!

With blessings and love,

-Your Earth Mother-

XIII. Native Wisdom

For all the understandably fearful coverage of
COVID-19 by the media, there is one narrative that
has been mostly ignored: the tremendous suffering
being felt by indigenous tribes around the world. As
horrible as the pandemic has been for all groups of
people, its impact has been even more devastating for
indigenous communities. Since the start of the
outbreak in the Americas, tribal peoples have
consistently had the highest hospitalization and death
rates. For example, in the United States, the virus has
severely impacted proud tribes like the Hopi, Navajo,
and Sioux. An already precarious situation for the first
peoples has steadily become a matter of cultural

survival. Each death of a tribal elder represents the loss of invaluable knowledge of traditional language and medicine. At the very moment when we are most in need of their wisdom native cultures are once again threatened by the specter of a horrifying disease. The world now yearns for the kind of wise counsel offered by indigenous elders like Myrtle Driver, a highly revered woman of the Eastern Band of Cherokee Indians in the Great Smoky Mountains of North Carolina. Her story is revealing for the hope that it might inspire.

Myrtle, who is a dear friend and teacher in my life, perfectly represents the gift of wisdom that we need in these trying times. She has devoted her entire life to spiritually uplifting and guiding her people. She has also been something of a pioneer in her tribe for keeping the traditional Cherokee language (the Cherokee Syllabary) alive. Toward this end, Myrtle has translated multiple children's books, such as Charlotte's Web, into her native tongue. She is also a traditional healer (a remarkable one at that) and has counseled incarcerated Cherokee youth and adults who have followed a wayward path.

Aside from her unsurmountable courage and selflessness, Myrtle carries herself with the utmost grace, dignity, humility, and wisdom. Despite being honored as a "Beloved Woman" (the highest honor that a Cherokee man or woman can receive) by the tribe for her tireless commitment to her people, she sincerely brushes aside all compliments. She is as humble as the roots of the glorious mountain laurels and rhododendrons that blanket the mountainous landscape of her tribe of survivors. Myrtle is as authentically devoted to the spirit of oneness as one can be and she has a rascally sense of humor. I should know.... as I have been on the butt end of her jokes far too many times to count!

Without trying to overly romanticize Indigenous cultures, (rampant poverty, drug addiction, and crime sadly persists on many reservations) Driver represents the essence of Indigenous values that I have also witnessed on other reservations like the Hopi. Those values are community, compassion, selflessness, courage, humility, and faith. But standing front and center in the indigenous belief system is that Earth is the supreme source of insight, revelation, and divine guidance. These values are in direct contrast to our culture's guiding values.

Instead of honoring family, our dominant culture extolls the supremacy of the individual above all else. In place of true compassion, our society often promotes a very selfish mindset. Courage is, unfortunately, something we also pay lip service to in bombastic political speeches and public service announcements but is rarely embodied by the actions of our leaders. Hubris, particularly in the more powerful nations, is also an unfortunate driving motivation for our rulers. Even amid an unprecedented global health crisis, we still hear arrogant slogans from our leaders like: "America

First". Why should one nation be deemed more important than any other nation? Why should we focus our energies on generating division?

In today's world, faith is also hard to come by. Sadly, many people living through these times have concluded that this nation (and maybe the entire world) is in a state of total collapse and that our future looks bleak. Understandably, the shock of a major pandemic, runaway unemployment, and social unrest is a lot to digest emotionally. It is crystal clear that the vision of indigenous cultures is very much needed right now. The original peoples have long known the correct way to live. It is now time to follow their example. The first thing we can all do is to raise awareness at how close we are to losing their remarkable wisdom and guidance at this time of unspeakable tragedy. The second thing that we can do is to help revive their vision of wisdom and love within the context of these times that we are living in.

Forrest Rivers

XIIII. Reviving an Old Vision for a New World

COVID-19 has opened a unique window for seekers of truth to put forward a vision for humanity that is conducive to the challenging times that we are living in. Ideally, this vision should build upon the indigenous values that we have recklessly strayed away from. Crises, like the kind that we are now confronting, tend to be the best of times to enact lasting change because the darkness of suffering has a way of pushing us into the light of new beginnings. The type of vision that we might imagine building is of a brotherhood of compassionate beings who work for the soulful uplift of all humanity. This vision would be rooted in the *Golden Rule* which states: "Do unto others as you would have them do to you." In such a vision, our conscious exercise of free will would prevail and the plundering of the Earth would not be tolerated. Everyone would also honor all forms of worship and channels of connecting to the One. The existence of different traditions would simply be regarded as multiple paths leading to the same mountain top of personal empowerment and transformation

In this vision, there would be no need to discuss the abstraction of "individual rights", because there would be no need to define what we were already free to say and to do. And rather than identify people by their occupations, we would dissolve our consumer identities and come to know our own Buddha-nature. To meet our basic needs like shelter and food, we would all be encouraged to be radically self-sufficient. Yet, we would also be intimately tied to our communities through small scale systems of sustainable agriculture. The value of how we earn our living would not be measured by such foolish standards as income, prestige, and academic degrees. Instead, the value of our work would be determined by how it contributes to the relief of suffering and the betterment of humanity.

In this vision, we would all heed the wisdom of an unnamed sage who once profoundly said: "The mind is a wonderful servant but a terrible master." In this painting of a resplendent future, children would be taught to meditate and pray from a young age and they would learn to see through the mind's compulsive habit of producing separation. Intuition would come to be known as the true staff of life and the mind would only be at its service. No longer would the blind be leading the blind because everyone would have received their spiritual vision.

The horrors of poverty, war, and division would be read about as hard lessons in humanity's conscious evolution. All students would be taught about the beliefs of native traditions to ground us in our

83

common roots of being. Men and women from all walks of life would live by the axiom that says: "democracies die when the arts cease to flourish." Accordingly, all would be actively encouraged to pursue creative passions like painting, writing, and music. Can these times really propel the human race forward in a new direction of oneness? Will these times be remembered for pushing us forward into a new age of love?

The choice to ascend into this state of "interbeing", as Zen Master, Thich Nhat Hahn describes it, is entirely up to us as empowered and capable individuals. How many of us have surveyed the state of the world at this moment and thought: "There has to be a better way?" I'm sure many have thought this. Be rest assured, there is a better way!

XV. Real Democracy

Monday, May 25, 2020, is a date that will forever be engrained in our consciousness as one when many people finally said, "enough is enough!" On that fateful day, George Floyd, an unarmed black man, was horrifically killed by a white Minneapolis police officer in broad daylight while bystanders pleaded with the officer for over eight minutes to release his knee hold from Floyd's neck. Floyd's death, one of the latest high-profile police killings of black people, immediately touched off a fury of protests and riots in major cities across America and throughout the world. In the very first days of the unrest, it became obvious what the twin-issues were for protesters: systemic racism in law enforcement and unaccountable police power.

As the protests gained momentum through the summer of 2020, it became apparent that the protesters were also demanding attention on an equally pressing issue: the practice of real democracy. Unknowingly, or not, countless men and women in the streets were pointing out the hypocrisy of America calling itself a democracy while systemically oppressing racial minorities. From a spiritual standpoint, too, the mostly peaceful protests were a profound testament to the power and courage of the human soul. As the police responded to these protests with the sadly predictable force of a totalitarian nation, many began to reflect on the crucial link between real democracy and spirituality. These protests have taught us that one cannot exist without the other. They are mutually reinforcing principles of compassion in action. The spiritual values of peace, unity, and love are the foundations of a sustainable and real democracy. In turn, real democracy is the external reflection of those same foundational values put into action.

Without question, COVID-19 has revealed many contradictions in the United States calling itself a democracy. From the open swindling of taxpayers by large corporations through legislation designed as "aid" to American small businesses, to the US Government's own shameful downplaying of a serious public health crisis to protect political interests, as well as the overwhelming burden of the government ordered shutdowns on the poor and vulnerable, all showed how America falls well short of being called a democracy. However, the killing of George Floyd and the response to the protests by those in power showed beyond a shadow of a doubt, that we are not one. This begs the question: What would real democracy in a post-COVID world even look like?

A real democracy would achieve five chief things. First and foremost, it would secure a true and lasting peace between people from all walks of life, between families, between communities, and between nations. This first expectation of a real democracy should really go without saying. If democracy cannot achieve universal peace what is the point of singing its praises at all? Is it any coincidence that all of the greatest social revolutionaries throughout history have sought to link the attainment of peace with the practice of real democracy? The Reverend Martin Luther King Jr, Mahatma Gandhi, and Nelson Mandela each routinely pointed out in their speeches that peace and the ideal of real democracy should go hand in hand. Gandhi, a man of deep faith, and the inspirational leader of India's struggle for independence went as far to say:

> "The true democrat is he who with purely nonviolent means defends his liberty and, therefore, his country's and ultimately that of the whole of mankind."

Second, in a real democracy, our leaders would be humble servants who embody the highest qualities of moral character. Leaders in a real democracy would probably draw motivation from such indigenous democratic traditions like the Iroquois Confederacy. In that Native-American compact (designed in the 1400s for mutual cooperation and self-defense between six neighboring tribes in upstate-New York and Pennsylvania), two male representative leaders were chosen from each of the six tribes by female elders. These leaders were selected based on the demonstrated qualities of wisdom, compassion, courage, and selflessness. While in power, these men were expected to give up all their worldly personal possessions and live with fewer material privileges than the average member of their tribe. They were also expected to inform their decisions with calm deliberation and were explicitly warned by their elders to refrain from any conflicts of interest. This was all to ensure genuine pureness of heart among their chosen leaders. On the whole, do our own leaders measure up to these lofty but attainable standards of leadership?

Third, in a real democracy, all people would enjoy the unlimited freedom of thought, individual expression, and right to religious worship. No one's thoughts would be manipulated by deceptive media outlets in service of the rich and powerful. Not one person's freedom of expression would be silenced by government authorities. Perhaps, most vital of all, the freedom to explore the depths of one's consciousness would be absolute. Even controversial methods of communing with the Divine such as using sacred entheogenic plants and substances would be fully protected and seen yet another gateway to connect to God.

Fourth, in a real democracy full equality would be enjoyed by all people regardless of such distinctions as class, race, religion, ethnicity, gender, sexual orientation, and political ideology. In such a state of being, there would be no need for so-called, "social justice warriors," because a true commitment to the celebration of diversity would already prevail in the hearts and minds of all people. In a real democracy, equality would be rooted in the noblest of passions among the people because the illusionary barriers of "us" and "them" would be broken down to reveal only "we."

Finally, in a real democracy, the genuine spirit of goodwill would underlie all of our meaningful interactions with one another and inform our collective decisions on issues of crucial importance. The people themselves, gathered in citizen assemblies of one form or another, would directly arrive at consensus-driven decisions (direct democracy) with only the welfare of their immediate communities in mind. The pursuit of individual self-interest would be discouraged within such self-governing circles as people began to see what the Russian anarchist philosopher, Peter Kropotkin, described as the virtues of "mutual aid," societies....

where cooperation not competition is seen as the key to our survival.

This period of crisis has afforded us all with the rare opportunity to imagine what a real democracy might soon look like. In the meanwhile, it would serve us well to be aware of how far we still have yet to go to achieve the exterior reflection of our inner awakening of spirit.

XVI. A More Fulfilling Economy

Otis and Savannah, a counterculture couple who are good friends of mine, were two of the untold millions who lost their jobs when the nationwide shutdowns began. Like most workers who filed for unemployment compensation during this time, the couple received uncharacteristically generous benefits (For America at least) that easily covered their basic household expenses. With ample time off and with their needs met, Otis and Savannah focused on becoming more independent from the economic system that they both see as excessively exploitive and in their own words, "soul-crushing". On her end, Savannah began producing her own herbal remedies and various creams from common medicinal plants and fungi found in the Southern Appalachian Mountains like Mullein and the Reishi mushroom. Otis, too, has been busy harvesting Cannabis for sale on the market.

The couple explained to me that they have sold and bartered their products on the local market and they expressed how much joy it has brought them to work for themselves, support their local economy, and provide sustainably made and healthy goods for their community. Otis and Savannah's uplifting story of declaring their economic independence from "the man", has only grown in popularity during this period of crisis. Stories like theirs, represent an admission that our present-day economy is broken.

Many other friends and acquaintances who I have spoken to during the pandemic, shared a similar desire as Otis and Savannah to break away from the system. Dylan and Mackenzie, another couple who are friends of mine, have taken the liberty during COVID to begin working toward their dream of starting their own sustainable and organic farm. Others, I spoke to also shared their dream of earning a living with their art and donating their time to humanitarian causes. Still, other individuals like Samuel, a beloved friend and spiritual mentor of mine, intends to create an off the grid nature healing refuge on the large acreage that he and his wife purchased in New Hampshire.

The connecting strand among the many inspiring beings I spoke to is to find a deeper meaning in their lives. All who shared their thoughts with me were highly aware of the fact that the way one earns their living must also align with such a deeper sense of purpose. This is not to say that our work should define us in the traditional way that we have been taught to believe. Rather, it is to say that when our work is rooted in something more authentic than just punching away at the clock it becomes a living statement of hope and greater fulfillment.

Ironically, one of the greatest and unintended gifts from governments (during this crisis) was that the paid time off from our jobs provided many people with the opportunity to temporarily escape from the "rat race". This time away has helped some dare to imagine a better way to re-align our work with a greater spiritual vision. For many, such a re-alignment means to actively participate in a small-scale economy where the meeting of one's basic needs and those of our communities come before profit. It also means engaging in work that meaningfully contributes to the peaceful uplift of humanity. Finally, re-aligning one's work with a greater spiritual vision also means engaging in labor that doesn't leave a footprint on our beautiful green Earth. Rather than desecrate and exploit her, as our current economic system does to an appalling degree, we must honor and serve her through the labor that we perform.

If we have learned anything from the fallout of COVID-19, it is that our imaginations have no limit. So, let us all imagine a more constructive way of relating to both the Earth and one another through choosing wisely how we spend our time working. We can all make the conscious choice to opt-out of the current economic paradigm of "what can I get for me", and instead promote sustainable alternatives that fill our lives with joy and a genuine devotion to the community. When we do this, we all become conscientious resisters of a system that we all know in our hearts is a racket to protect the interests of the rich and powerful.

After all, there is no reason why (as of this book's publication) the top one percent of wealthiest people in America should control 40 percent of the nation's wealth and the bottom 80 percent (the majority of us) only 8 percent. There are also no acceptable reasons why 1 in 6 children in the wealthiest nation on Earth should face food insecurity while the super-rich retreat to their multiple vacation homes on private jets. The lack of real democracy and a failing economic system are prime reasons for our collective suffering. But we all have the power to set into motion a revival of more deeply spiritual ways of relating to the Earth and the rest of humanity. A return to religion's roots is what is needed to set such a vision into motion.

XVII. Back to Religion's Roots

The multiple crises that we face demand a response from our religious traditions. However, the religion we know as an institutionalized hierarchy of powerful leaders and their followers will no longer serve us. It may only exasperate our problems even more. We must return to religion's roots. We need the inspiring wisdom of a Jesus or a Mohammad without the corrupt guidance of religious authorities. We need to touch the transcendent beauty of the Hindu or Jewish scriptures, first hand, through one-pointed meditation. And we must see our own Buddha-nature reflected in the life-giving rivers that flow effortlessly to the infinite ocean. Direct religious experience is the

99

panacea to the deep-seated troubles of our times. For in truth, COVID-19 and all the related problems that it has brought to the surface are indicators of a deeper spiritual crisis at hand.

At the roots of all the world's major religions are mystical traditions that emphasize the importance of one's direct and intuitive experience in connecting to the greater reality. In Christianity, these roots are discovered through the lives and works of mystics like Saint Francis, Saint Teresa of Calcutta, and Thomas Merton. In Islam, their mystical tradition is expressed through practices like Sufi Dancing and through the words of poet sages such as Rumi and Hafiz. In Buddhism, it is found through Zen, a school of wisdom described by some as the "gateless gate", in which seekers arrive at their own enlightenment through persistent meditation (Zazen) and less reliance on the word of scripture. In Hinduism, this mystical tradition is reflected in sacred texts like the Upanishads and the Bhagavad Gita. It is also experienced by the many wandering Sadhus (holy men) in search of an unfettered communion with Brahman (God). Finally, in Judaism, the mysterious Kabbalah is a powerful and fascinating mystical expression of that faith.

Aldous Huxley, the revered writer-sage, calls these common mystical ties in all religions the "perennial philosophy". Whatever name we use to describe it, our mystical traditions have the power to transform entire societies because they can change the hearts of all individuals from the inside out. On that point, consider this revealing quote from Gary Snyder, the great beat poet:

> "The practice of meditation, for which one needs only the ground beneath one's feet, wipes out mountains of junk being pumped into the mind by the mass media and supermarket universities. The belief in a serene and generous fulfillment of natural loving desires is strengthened by meditation and destroys ideologies which blind, maim, and repress."

As we have seen, the type of direct spiritual experience(meditation) that Snyder writes passionately about has the positive effect of raising both our individual and collective states of consciousness. More significantly, direct spiritual seeking has the power to heal the division between groups of people and build peace among all God's children. Whenever we meditate or pray, we can't help but feel a deep kinship with all beings of the Earth. It is this profound sense of interconnection that sparks monumental shifts in consciousness and breaks down barriers of separation. It is the illusion of separation that frustrates our attempts at peace in the first place. Anthropocentrism, racism, sexism, nationalism, and classism are all faces of a false reality that pictures the web of being as a collection of unrelated parts.

As the Chandogya Upanishad from the Hindu tradition, reminds us, direct spiritual seeking helps us come to a unitive vision of reality:

"The self is hidden in the lotus of the heart. Those who see themselves in all creatures go day by day into the world of Brahman hidden in the heart. Established in peace, they rise above body-consciousness to the supreme light of the Self. Immortal, free from fear, this Self is Brahman, called the True. Beyond the mortal and the immortal, he binds both worlds together. Those who know this live day after day in heaven in this life."

Returning to religion's roots (Huxley's perennial philosophy) is one way to heal the discord that is escalating in even once stable nations like America. There, tensions between so-called "conservatives" and "liberals" have reached such a boiling point that some mainstream pundits on both sides have even opined that a second civil war is inevitable. The events surrounding COVID-19 have taken this "culture war" to new and alarming heights. Strongly clashing perspectives between the two groups have only intensified. Everything from the government's response to the handling of the pandemic, to the enforcement of wearing masks in public, to sharply differing opinions about Black Lives Matter have been called into question.

If this fire of division isn't soon extinguished, it could easily spill over into more violent conflict. Sadly, every day, more and more Americans continue to break off into one of the two extreme camps of "far-right" and "far-left". As this shift takes place, the number of people standing on neutral ground steadily declines and we become a nation of extremists. The negative consequences of this deepening polarization are there for us all to see:

dissolved friendships, broken marriages, shocking displays of intolerance, and deadly clashes between protesters and police. More now than ever we must embrace what unites us. The mystical traditions---our forgotten spiritual roots---are our great refuge in these times of moral fragmentation. Black Elk, a very wise Native-American mystic and a beloved leader of the

Oglala Lakota, said peace between groups of people and between nations cannot be attained until each first finds their own inner peace:

> "The first peace, which is the most important, is that which comes within the souls of people when they realize their relationship, their oneness, with the universe and all its powers, and when they realize that at the center of the universe dwells Wakan-Tanka and that this center is really everywhere, it is within each of us. This is the real peace, and the others are but reflections of this. The second peace is that which is made between two individuals, and the third is that which is made between two nations. But above all, you should understand that there can never be peace between nations until there is known that true peace, which, as I have often said, is within the souls of men".

Happily, the roots of our mystical traditions can help guide us through this period of immense suffering and help reveal the peace that Black Elk always knew was within us.

Forrest Rivers

XVIII. The Promise of Self-Sufficiency

In 1967, before a gathering of hippie youth in San Francisco, CA, Timothy Leary coined a phrase that perfectly captured the mindset of an entire generation. The phrase was, "Turn on, tune in, drop out." In just six words, this counterculture icon powerfully conveyed a message of direct spiritual seeking and non-engagement with the dominant culture. If one lives by the wisdom of this phrase, they will inevitably find themselves standing on the outside looking in at society. This reality begs the following question: What is a seeker of truth supposed to do when their consciousness expands so dramatically that compliance with the values of their culture are no longer possible?

The answer is that you must become self-sufficient in both thought and action. The thought part means tuning your mind to the truth within and not to what is being propagandized on the outside. The action part means doing things like growing your own food, building your own home, collecting your own rainwater, and finding an alternative energy source to power your community. It also means working out an independent and workable system of direct democracy and being a participant in a more local, just, and sustainable economy. Being truly self-sufficient in both thought and action go hand in hand. The move to become so in action is born from free and independent thought that sees a different way of relating to the world as possible.

Stephen Gaskin, the late co-founder of The Farm (founded in 1971), a well-known and remarkable off the grid hippie community in Summertown,

Tennessee, once said the following about the promise of self-sufficiency in his delightful book <u>This Season's People</u>:

> "It is revolutionary growing your own food instead of supporting the profit system. It is revolutionary to deliver your own babies instead of paying thousands of dollars a head to profit-oriented hospitals and doctors. It is revolutionary to get the knowledge out of college and make it so you don't have to sell your soul to learn something. It is revolutionary to learn how to fix stuff, rather than junk it or take it in to be replaced."

For Gaskin, the Farm's successful experiment in living Leary's wisdom was itself a profound expression of opposition to our dependency on society. In many ways, the event of COVID-19 has revealed the extent to which most of us are not at all self-sufficient in the ways that both Leary and especially Gaskin imagined. Indeed, the first few months of the pandemic showed just how reliant we still are on big corporations and governments. A dramatic example was the overwhelming fear among many that grocery stores would run out of food.

This irrational fear, driven by our dependence on the commercial for-profit food system, subsequently led to mass panic shopping not just in the United States but across the world as well. On a side note.... the pandemic has taught us that if you want to witness the breakdown of modern society just threaten to shut down its food markets! The staggering number of Americans who (out of necessity) had little choice but to file for unemployment benefits when the shutdowns began was another example of our lack of self-sufficiency.

Thankfully, this age of COVID has delivered two revelations as they relate to self-sufficiency. The first revelation is that becoming so is highly possible now in this age of ever sophisticated channels of communication through the internet. Today, one can literally pick up any practical skill such as building a tiny home, canning food, or installing solar panels on their house. No longer do we even need to go into the military or become an apprentice to acquire the very skills that we can now learn through our phones and computers. A second and even more inspiring revelation is that becoming self-sufficient is food for our souls. There is something inherently beneficial to our own spiritual growth when we learn to be so. For one, we become more confidant and able beings when we gain the skills needed for our own survival. The struggle in learning these new talents also makes us more self- resilient in the face of navigating obstacles along the way. We also find gratitude when we add new skills to our repertoire. Becoming self-sufficient will also inevitably deepen our relationship and sense of connection with the Earth. Practices like farming, foraging, and building shelters have the effect of reverting us into a state of communion with the earth and all her natural cycles.

Not long ago, I spent an extremely hot summer (even by Southern Appalachian standards!) working on a hemp farm in the mountains of North Carolina. Much of the work I did in the field was physically exhausting. Yet, despite enduring the hard labor and many pains in my body, I recall feeling strangely fulfilled while working there. I was learning how to farm, getting my hands dirty, and putting in an honest day's work. Furthermore, as the weeks went by my bond with the land and surrounding mountains grew stronger. So much so, that the farm began to feel like an extension of my being. As the cannabis plants began to mature, my connection to the land only heightened. While working on the farm I began to truly understand what my old-time farmer friend, Rick, had meant when he once told me that he "feels closest to Christ" when he works the land behind his home. What I discovered in that summer on the farm is that learning self-sufficient skills not only makes us feel more confidant, able, resilient, and fully connected beings but it also brings peace of mind.

In the end, becoming self-sufficient in action requires that we first become it in thought. To this point, G.I. Gurdjieff, the Greek-Armenian spiritual teacher, said the following:

> "If you wish to get out of prison the first thing you must do is realize that you are in prison. If you think you are free, you can't escape."

If we continue to think we need the mass corporate machine to feed and supply us with our life necessities, then we will remain locked in our own prison of dependency believing we are free. The same idea applies to our relationship with our governments. The more we think we need their financial assistance the more reliant we will be on our manipulative rulers who want us to remain dependent. These times are ripe to pursue the promise of self-sufficiency in thought and in action. "Turn On, Tune In, Drop Out"

may well become the mantra of yet another generation!

XVIIII. The Message

As a child, I always had fun imagining that I found a message in a bottle washed up on shore. I liked to picture what that letter might say. Would it be an offering of hope? Or might it be a critique of the world imploring us to do better? Maybe, the note would contain instructions from an enlightened sage on how to live more wisely? Then again, what if it said nothing at all? Maybe a blank piece of paper would be all that was needed to inspire our imaginations to finish the script in accord with our soul's deepest wishes and desires.

The following is a message that I would imagine a beachgoer discovering and reading long after the events surrounding COVID-19 have receded into the ocean mist of our awareness. As you contemplate your own experience living through these tumultuous times, what would your message to future generations be?

"A Message to Humanity"

Dear Lovers, seekers, and humble explorers of the Great Mystery,

I write to you from the year 2020. You may know it in your history books as the year that all hell broke loose, and the world turned! In truth, multiple crises have defined this time and have left some questioning if this period might ominously mark the end of days for humanity. Despite all our advanced technologies and scientific prowess, we have been unable to control the outbreak of a virus that has wreaked havoc on much of the world's population. Despite our arrogant proclamations of being culturally superior and progressive socially, our leaders have also been unable to prevent much of the Earth's inhabitants from sliding into dire poverty as this pandemic unfolds.

This most bizarre and chaotic year has also marked the start of a mass wave of resistance movements across the world against various forms of tyranny and oppression. Much of this resistance has been decidedly peaceful and non-violent. However, you should know, that calls by political extremists for armed and violent protests have increasingly grown in numbers flouting the great wisdom of Jesus that says:

> "You have heard that it was said, 'Eye for eye, and tooth for tooth.'[a] 39 But I tell you, do not resist an evil person. If anyone slaps you on the right cheek, turn to them the other cheek also."

Sadly, as the world's attention is consumed by these multiple crises, commercial predators continue to desecrate our own Earth Mother and the cultures of her brave indigenous protectors on a scale never seen. It is resoundingly clear that we must learn how to honor and live as one with the Earth if we wish to stave off our own extinction. Dear reader, my intent is not to scare you or bring you down with troubling words. I am just trying to be honest with you about the true state of our world at the moment.

In these times, too many people appear to be proud of their woeful ignorance and wear it like a badge of honor to justify unspeakable acts of horror against their own brothers and sisters. The disease of selfishness that currently plagues the world is at least as concerning as the actual spread of the virus itself. The illusion of separation must be overcome.

Lest you think that 2020 has been all doom and gloom, simmering just beneath the surface is a powerful movement of higher consciousness. Everywhere across the globe people are looking within to seek solutions to the problems we collectively face. Many awakening souls are now just coming to the profound realization that inner wisdom, not conceptual knowledge is what is needed at this moment of the dark night of our souls. Can you imagine how wonderfully we could all live if we put as much effort into truly knowing ourselves as we do in making money and consuming?

While it might be difficult for many in our generation to imagine such an alternative reality in this age of ego run amok, I can only hope that the inspiring values of peace and love now finally prevail in the culture that you, humble reader, lives in. Something deep within me says that the events of 2020 represented a dramatic point of departure for the conscious evolution of humanity. Like many people around the world, I felt frightened when all these unsettling events began happening in quick succession of one another. For a moment, I even pondered if the biblical "end of times" were truly upon us. But then I closed my eyes and I clearly saw what up until that instant had escaped me: that these are only a metaphorical end of times in terms of how we relate to ourselves, one another, and to the Earth. These events have provided us the spiritual fire to transition from a lower state of soul awareness into a higher one. Only through darkness can the light emerge. Only through suffering can the wheel of karma turn to fully know the true joy of being.

In this moment of awakening, may all the world's great messengers converge to deliver the universal message of peace and oneness that this world so desperately needs!

Om Shanti. Om Shanti. Om Shanti.

XX. An Art Renaissance

In times of great social upheaval, all human beings (whether conscious of this fact or not) are challenged to question the very meaning of their existence. Events such as war, economic collapse, pandemics, political revolution, and natural disasters have the effect of shaking men and women out of their day-to-day routines and sense of comfort. As history clearly shows, these ages have also sparked some of the most profound and inspiring renaissances in the creative arts like music, writing, and painting. Periods of social upheaval and soulful expression fit together seamlessly. Just as we cannot separate the river's journey from its destination of the vast blue ocean, so can't we separate revolutions in the creative arts from their societal contexts. As a case in point, consider the

Renaissance of art that took place during the decades of the 1960s and '70s.

In a global context, this age had it all. A hugely unpopular and devastating war in Vietnam, the cold war and the looming threat of nuclear devastation, independence movements in Africa and the Civil Rights Movement in the United States, women's Liberation on both sides of the Atlantic, as well as multiple indigenous rights' movements in the Americas. In short, for much of the world social revolution and war came to define that period's external landscape. Unquestionably, the escalation of extreme government violence amid a backdrop of mass protests and growing existential fears gave rise to an inspiring movement of higher consciousness that became embodied by the hippie counterculture. At its core, the hippies were at the forefront of a spiritual movement that sought to promote a more soulful and natural way of living in harmony with the whole of Creation. On the surface, they saw an external world marked by widespread fear, greed, mindless conformity. and hypocrisy.

In response to society's madness, the hippies turned within through such inner outlets as meditation, the use of psychedelics, and communing with nature. This great period of inner searching saw an explosion of raw creativity that simultaneously served as a deep social commentary of the unjust nature of society while also sharing hopeful visions of transcended states of awareness.

The hippies' powerful merging of an outer world critique and an inner vision of untapped hope, peace, and unity found its soulful expression most powerfully through music. Household acts like the Beatles, Bob Marley, Jimi Hendrix, Pink Floyd, Led Zeppelin, The Who, Jefferson Airplane, Janis Joplin, Bob Dylan, Neil Young, The Doors, and the Grateful Dead communicated the hippie ethos through the vehicle of sound. But this era's renaissance in art was not limited to music alone. Beatnik poets and

123

counterculture authors like Alan Ginsberg, Jack Kerouac, William Burroughs, Ken Kesey, and Gary Snyder accomplished through words what musicians did through music. And who can fail to mention (perhaps) three of the most impactful and sage-like writers of that generation: Baba Ram Dass, Aldous Huxley, and Alan Watts!

At the present moment, the world is primed for the latest renaissance of art. This spark of expression may even eclipse the creative genius of the hippie counterculture from a half-century ago. So far, the events and happenings of our times are providing the ultimate context for a tidal wave of creativity. The opportunity presented by COVID-19 for such a widespread expression of higher consciousness cannot be overstated. There is absolutely no doubt that this pandemic has been terribly tragic in terms of human life lost. However, it is precisely the presence of death's now very public face that has sparked inner reflection on our own mortality. In essence, COVID-19 has forced all of humanity to at once confront that one mysterious yet omnipresent constant that colors our very existence. For the first time in decades, the majority of humans are suddenly forced to examine the tough existential questions that are typically buried beneath our society's techno-consumerist distractions. Some of these questions have consumed the minds of philosophers and the souls of mystics from every spiritual faith: "Who am I"? "What happens when I die"? "Will I be reborn"? "What is my purpose here on Earth"? "Who or What is God"?" Undoubtedly, many beings will feel drawn to the creative arts to express their own answers to such deep and existential questions.

There is an additional layer to this pandemic that has lent itself to the coming renaissance of art. In a desperate attempt to contain this virus, governments around the world carried out unprecedented shutdowns of several key industries. The impact caused by them has had far-reaching and unforeseen consequences for humanity. On the one hand, the massive shutdowns facilitated the full-scale meltdown of the global financial system and led to an unemployment crisis not seen since the height of the Great Depression. Predictably, the shock to the economy has exasperated our collective fear and inflicted significant hardships on the majority of workers and the poor. On the other hand, due to subsequent rounds of "social distancing" and home quarantining most of the world's population have found more time for solitude than ever before. This added alone time has been a catalyst for spirited self-reflection. Inevitably, remarkable works of art will be one of the positive outcomes from this period of isolation.

While the world grapples with the severity of this crisis and all it portends for the future of humanity; deep and long-standing systemic problems have been fully exposed for us all to see. Such problems include the continuous tax-funded government bailouts of greedy corporations, politicians who use their elite insider knowledge to profit amid periods of crisis, soaring wealth inequality between the rich and poor, systemic racism, and a pattern of pathological lies peddled to the public by self-interested leaders and media sources. The outbreak of COVID-19 has dramatically revealed that immoral values like greed, violence, fear, and division currently underlie the foundations of the global- financial system.

In the days and months ahead, we can expect many peaceful souls to do what their forebearers did during the hippie counterculture. The era of a new renaissance in art is upon us. To all artists and creative souls, the time has come to do what you do best: CREATE, MOVE, and INSPIRE! Through your art, reveal the absurdity of organizing our societies around the worst aspects of the human condition. Even more important.... convey through your creativity the hope that exists in recognizing that death is not to

127

be feared, that love will always prevail, and that all things in this marvelous universe are intimately connected as one. In these times of shared suffering, the reality of our eternal oneness has never been more apparent than it is now. Always remember that conveying the truth of our cosmic unity serves the highest and noblest aims of creative expression. The artists of this generation are poised to become some of our greatest warriors in the spiritual war that is now upon us.

XXI. A Spiritual War

When we hear the word "war", we typically think of a conquering army, innocent people being killed, or the awful images of physically and emotionally broken veterans returning home from battle. However, in metaphysical reality, the meaning of war deepens. Metaphysically speaking, one could interpret all worldly phenomena as manifestations of the spiritual plane. We are all just actors in an incomprehensibly wondrous cosmic screenplay (what Hindus call Lila). This belief, as many followers of

129

eastern religions, espouse, points to a world where we have all been divinely assigned unique roles (in physical form) in agreement with our karma. We assume these roles in a way that reflects the present interaction of all contending forces in the Universe and their eternal quest to achieve balance.

According to this same eastern worldview, no dueling forces in the cosmos are actually in any real conflict. Light and dark forces, good and evil energies, as well as ego and spirit ONLY APPEAR to be in direct conflict to us from where we are standing. In our culture of "black and white" dualities, we tend to dismiss the unitive nature of seeming polarities. In reality dark is needed to bring light, evil must be realized to know the meaning of good, one must first be ignorant to be wise, and all of us must transcend the vanity of ego before we can taste the sparkling springs of spirit. In a metaphysical sense war is not strictly a conflict of opposing forces that takes place outside us. Rather, it is also a contest between the prevailing forces of nature within us.

This "inner war" is akin to the kind described in the epoch Hindu classic: The Bhagavad Gita. In that sacred book, the great warrior Arjuna is encouraged to fight a spiritual war within by Krishna, charioteer, and God incarnate in disguise. To be sure, the setting of the Gita takes place on an actual physical battlefield. However, the real theme of this story is the war within oneself.

In the "Gita", Krishna instructs his faithful disciple Arjuna on how to achieve self-realization. From the onset of this incredibly beautiful and moving scripture, Krishna equates the pursuit of self-realization with the surrender of one's own ego before God. Of course, Krishna represents one unique and perfect manifestation of the Godhead (Brahman) in form. It is fitting, then, that he also encourages Arjuna to give up all selfish craving and focus his devotion on him:

"All those who take refuge in me, whatever their birth, race, sex, or caste, will attain the same goal; this realization can be attained even by those whom society scorns. Therefore, having been born in this transient and forlorn world, give all your love to me. Fill your mind with me; love me; serve me; worship me always. Seeking me in your heart, you will, at last, be united with me." (Bhagavad Gita)

Arjuna represents the perfect disciple through his unwavering faith and devotion to Krishna. Yet, Krishna still cautions this great warrior about the pitfalls on the path to self-realization. In order to break free from the hellish grip of ego, all seekers must first learn how to still their minds through meditation and cultivate an attitude of detachment from the fruits of one's actions.

On his first point, Krishna is crystal clear as to why all sincere spiritual aspirants should try to practice meditation....to achieve self-realization:

"The Supreme Reality stands revealed in the consciousness of those who have conquered themselves. Those who aspire to the state of Yoga should seek the Self in inner solitude through meditation. With body and mind controlled they should constantly practice one-pointedness, free from expectations and attachment to material possessions. When meditation is mastered, the mind is unwavering like the flame of a lamp in a windless place. In the still mind, in the depths of meditation, the Self reveals itself. Beholding the Self by means of the Self, an aspirant knows the joy and peace of complete fulfillment." (Bhagavad Gita)

On Krishna's second point, he explains to Arjuna that devoting one's life to the path of selfless service (Karma yoga) is both the highest calling of mankind and the surest path to self-realization. To selflessly serve and fulfill one's "dharma" or personal destiny, all serious men and women on the path of spirit must first renounce the fruits of their actions. In other words, all beings must learn to act without expectation of worldly rewards or acknowledgments:

"Every selfless act, Arjuna, is born from
Brahman, the eternal, infinite Godhead.
Brahman is present in every act of service. All
life turns on this law. Those who violate it,
indulging the senses for their own pleasure and
ignoring the needs of others, have wasted their
life. You have the right to work, but never to the
fruits of work. The ignorant work for their own
profit, Arjuna, the wise work for the welfare of
the world, without thought for themselves.
Perform all work carefully, guided by
compassion." (Bhagavad Gita)

As a culture, COVID-19 has revealed just how
much we are truly engaged in a spiritual war between
the very forces of ego and spirit that Krishna
describes. Within this crisis, we have all seen direct
manifestations of this conflict played out on the
physical plane. One striking example was the anti-
mask movement in the United States and Great
Britain. Another was the shocking and reckless
decision by the leader of the former nation to hold

huge indoor political rallies against the overwhelming advice of the medical community. Do either of these examples reflect the spirit of self-realization that Krishna teaches? Would a self-realized being conclude that their right to not wear a mask in public outweighs the threat of getting others seriously sick or worse? Would a self-realized person in a position of immense influence decide that their need to stay in power is more important than the health and wellbeing of the very people they were sworn to always serve and protect? Is either example rooted in the spirit of selfless service? Do they reflect the surrender of the fruits of action before the higher power? These are indeed some heavy questions to ponder.

COVID-19 has shown the power of the ego's tremendous hold over our collective consciousness. However, at the same, we could not ask for a better set of external circumstances with which to work in this spiritual war. The pandemic landscape has provided us with ample opportunities for self-reflection and

135

selfless service. As an example, at the start of the shutdowns, I caught up with an old friend who has long struggled to overcome alcoholism. This individual told me that he credits COVID-19 with helping him quit drinking due to the time he has had to reflect on his own life path. Most inspiringly, he told me that through this period of home isolation he has realized that he wants to devote the rest of his days to serving others by becoming a substance abuse counselor. In the truest sense, this person is a spiritual warrior in the way that Sri Krishna imagined!

In a similar light, I also recall an email that I received from one of my students about two months into the outbreak long after the college had already shut down. This student wrote to me to say that the time away from campus has helped him realize that he wants to pursue a career that allows him to serve others. In pursuit of that goal, he indicated that he is giving up his plan to become a lawyer and instead wants to become a social worker that specializes in serving the homeless population. Needless to say, this email warmed my heart. One day in the not-so-distant future, we will all kick back in our chairs and reflect on 2020 and say that was the year when the spiritual war finally titled toward the forces of light. Call me naïve or idealistic, but I have a strong feeling that the power of the living spirit will prevail! Now tell me.... are you with me in thinking that we have the power to be the shapers of our destiny?

Forrest Rivers

XXII. Shapers of Our Destiny

I like to spend as much of my time as possible hiking in the mountains. The solitude, reflection, fresh air, and communion with nature are my favorite things about being out in the wild. The storied Appalachian Trail crosses within 20 minutes of the mountain town where I have lived for much of the past half-decade of my life or longer. Sometimes, while hiking on the "AT", as its affectionally called by Appalachian Trail hikers, I will encounter a "thru-hiker" (one attempting to hike the entire 2,181 trail end to end). I have found that stopping to talk to these hikers are always worth the brief intrusion into my own solo experience in nature. These individuals are filled with so much passion, dedication, and spirit that conversing with them never fails to uplift my own day.

Sometime in July 2020, about four months into the COVID-19 outbreak here in the US, I crossed paths with a thru-hiker on the AT up high on a local summit. As we introduced ourselves to one another he told me his name was "Noble." Noble was his given trail name (it is a time-honored tradition on the Appalachian Trail that every thru-hiker is given a trail name by another thru-hiker) and he went by that rather than his real moniker. He excitedly explained that this was his first attempt at hiking the AT but that he had successfully completed the other two major long-distance trails in the United States----the 2,650 mile Pacific Crest Trail (PCT) and the 3,100 mile Continental Divide Trail(CDT).

For Noble, completing the AT would earn him the very rare (only 440 hikers since 1994 have achieved the feat) and remarkably difficult honor of the "Triple Crown,". A Triple Crown is when a hiker completes each of the three major long-distance trails in the United States. Each of the efforts must be documented and the few who complete the monumental challenge are awarded with plaques of distinction each fall at a banquet organized by the Appalachian Long-Distance Hikers Association (ALDHA).

During our brief interaction, I remember asking Noble (who was 55 years old at the time and gave off the vibe of total inner peace) why he decided to attempt this inspiring feat amid a major pandemic that kept roughly 90 percent of the hikers who annually embark on the trek off the trail. A huge smile broke out across his face as he simply replied:

"Because it's my destiny and I am the shaper of it."

As one who tried his best to maintain safe practices during the pandemic, I couldn't help but reach out and give him a high five in response to his answer. After a few minutes, I wished him good luck on his incredible journey north to his final destination of Mount Katahdin in Maine. We then went our separate ways. All I could think about on my way back down the mountain to my car was his inspiring words: "because it's my destiny and I am the shaper of it."

I thought to myself how noble is a shining example of a being is who has stopped at nothing to achieve his soul's desire. His quest reminds me of a lot of Paulo Coelho's mystical character, Santiago, in the best-selling book The Alchemist. In that celebrated novel, Santiago goes on a long and epic pilgrimage in search of a hidden treasure only to discover that the journey, itself, was his real destiny. Noble's words and example should serve as inspiration in this period of extreme anxiety and fear. Overcoming both paralyzing emotions is especially challenging now and will continue to be so even after this pandemic has passed. After all, it is not as if we will go back to the "normal" that reigned pre-COVID. Very likely, much of the world will continue to live in fear of the next pandemic while others struggle to put their lives back together as a result of sickness, job loss, and other debilitating effects of the virus.

Noble's courage to undertake his own pilgrimage to nowhere and everywhere is also a powerful reminder that we, too, are shapers of our own destinies.... even during a moment in time when it appears that we have lost all control. Knowing this should fill you with great hope as we all attempt to navigate these rough and difficult waters. This storm shall pass, and you will be called upon to light the path to a brighter day. In the meantime, if the feeling of hopelessness should rear its ugly head think of Noble, the fearless hiker who is shaping his own destiny one step at a time....

XXIII. One World Healing

One day soon, the scientific community will inevitably discover an effective (and hopefully safe) vaccine for COVID-19 and this virus will come to be seen in the same way that we treat other once devastating diseases like Polio or Measles....as an exceedingly rare and highly controllable menace. However, just because we may soon bring this virus under control does not mean that we will immediately begin the healing process. This pandemic has inflicted such deep suffering on humanity that it may take years for us all to heal physically, emotionally, and spiritually. Aside from guaranteeing access to physical therapy for the countless millions who contracted serious cases of the virus, the aftermath of COVID-19 will also demand the creation of various outlets to facilitate our emotional and spiritual healing as well. The sheer trauma inflicted by this pandemic has been on such a wide scale that many people simply do not know how to process all that they have been through.

For those who lost a beloved family member or friend, the expansion of mental health services to help manage grief will be required. Increased access to substance abuse counselors will also need to be made available for those who suffered close and traumatic brushes with death. Even for those fortunate enough to not have contracted the disease or lost loved ones, the number of people suffering from an array of anxiety disorders will only swell as many contemplate their own mortality for the first time. Without the tools to effectively process all that we have been through, we cannot get on with the healing of the world.

From a spiritual standpoint, two incredibly positive things have emerged from this pandemic that will profoundly aid us in our healing. First, because the whole world has experienced this public health calamity together, we have fostered a collective sense of shared suffering. In essence, we can all meaningfully relate to the pain that many are feeling. As a result, we can keep our hearts open while creating one universal healing circle that encompasses the whole world. In numerous studies, mental health practitioners have shown just how crucial it is for patients in trauma recovery to have access to loving communities who can meaningfully relate to what they have been through.

In the context of our healing from COVID-19, it is truly a blessing then, that such a loving community comprised of nearly the entire globe is arising in the mutual aid of one another. In an inspiring fashion, we have entered an age, not unlike the period after World War II when we all had to confront our collective suffering together. The crucial difference this time around is that the planet is now connected in remarkable ways. The advent of the internet age has not only served to facilitate an unprecedented wave of communication across the earth, but it has also made the empathetic flow of our understanding possible. Due to 21st century technologies like smartphones and personal laptops, we can literally (in seconds) access the suffering being felt by our distant brothers and sisters. The ability to gain such an acute awareness of human suffering has also made it more conceivable than ever to unite and end that same sorrow.

Through this unprecedented use of global telecommunications, we have already gained significant insight into the extent of COVID-19 related suffering around the world. For example, we have all heard about and shared the horrifying stories of Italian hospitals that were forced to ration crucial lifesaving equipment and make heartbreaking decisions on who should live and who should die. We have also been made digital witnesses to the virus's devastating impact on the poorest citizens in both

India and Brazil. And of course, we have also watched in horror as the United States (supposedly the most medically and scientifically advanced nation in the world) epically botched their response to COVID-19. Is it really that difficult to imagine humanity using the very same technologies to facilitate the world's healing in the months and years ahead? And is it inconceivable to envision mass prayer circles emerging through expanded interface programs like Zoom? In a post COVID world, it is not hard to imagine widespread international exchange programs arising that combine mental health strategies and spiritual wisdom for healing. Truly, as never before, our shared suffering and healing are intertwined as one.

The world's unparalleled access to ancient healing practices is the second thing that will facilitate our collective healing. Thanks to the internet, the global population is now able to gain widespread exposure to natural and traditional teachings that have long been shown to reduce anxiety, heighten awareness, and promote inner peace. Access to such soulfully uplifting practices such as mindfulness meditation, art and sound therapy, yoga, and the conscious use of entheogenic plants and fungi (like psilocybin mushrooms) will unquestionably aid our healing in a most profound kind of way.

As the virus is brought under control and social distancing guidelines are gradually lifted, we will likely see more people drawn to therapeutic settings like the kind that I and Betty Mandeville, a former colleague of mine, started at Volunteer State Community College in Nashville, TN. Twice weekly, the two of us, a group of students, and other faculty met for an hour of guided meditation and contemplative sharing. These "peaceful gatherings", as we came to call them, not only promoted the exploration of higher consciousness but also facilitated the emotional and spiritual healing of all participants involved.

A post COVID world may also see the expansion of general wellness programs offered at local community centers, schools, workplaces, and even prisons. These wellness programs may wind up incorporating some combination of yoga, meditation, and alternative healing methods like acupuncture or tapping exercises. It is also possible that the already burgeoning field of wilderness therapy will continue to grow in popularity as victims of this pandemic-related trauma look to heal through re-connecting with the beauty of mother nature. It is also likely that a growing number of people will turn to creative outlets like music, poetry, and painting to help them find joy again. Our world's healing may very well coincide with the renaissance of art described in an earlier chapter.

In the end, this much is certain: our collective healing will bring us exponentially closer toward arriving at a greater understanding of both self and others.

XXIIII. To Be and To Love

One day during the height of the pandemic, I was sitting with Clay, a very dear and infinitely wise 72-year-old friend of mine. The two of us were basking in the spirit and talking about our connection to the One. At some point during the discussion, Clay turned to me with a big smile on his face and said in a knowing tone that the point of life was "to be and to love." The meaning of life he explained, was really that simple. According to my friend, there is never any need to over-intellectualize or philosophize about our existence. Rather, all we are called upon to do is to be and to love. Clay's words were such a revelation for me that when I got home that night I pulled out my journal and tried to sincerely recall all the times in my life when I experienced the bliss of just being and loving.

I thought back to the innocence of my childhood joyously playing capture the flag and basketball in the front yard with my friends without a care in the world. I thought of a poignant moment minutes before a high school track race when my father stood close behind me and showered me with unwavering love and support. I thought of the first day when I was finally off on my own in college and the overwhelming sense of freedom I felt. I thought of the day when Abbie, my beloved dog, and best friend, first came into my life and how I felt strangely certain that our meeting was more like a reunion of two souls over many lifetimes than the introduction it appeared on the surface to be.

I then thought of the countless times lying in bed with my kindred spirit, Rose, after making love and feeling overwhelmed by the incredible energy and warmth flowing between us. I thought of dancing at my first reggae show and feeling so connected to the music's sweet and soulful vibrations that I entered a trance-like state. I thought of numerous spirited hikes to the top of majestic peaks in both the Smoky and Rocky Mountains---- the two magical places where I have lived for most of the decade of my 30's. I thought of my first synchronistic meeting with Myrtle, the wise and godly Cherokee elder who would become a close friend and beloved teacher. I thought of a past trip to Maui, Hawaii, and how that island's astounding beauty had opened my heart and awakened my spirit. I thought of the immense gratitude I felt for having the opportunity to perform live music for a period with two of my closest friends as crowds gathered around to receive our positive message. I also thought of the chance encounter that I had with a red robbed monk in the middle of a Nashville, Tennessee greenway and the extraordinary presence of compassion and equanimity that he radiated. Many other untold moments passed freely from my pen to paper as I reflected.

What was it about those moments, I asked myself, that had made them so memorable? Each of these moments brought me into the totality of being fully present with my heart wide open to the wonder of existence. In those precious instances, it is as if my mind stopped clinging to what the next sequence in my life would be. Instead of my mind being someplace else, I was just here, swimming in an ocean of pure awareness. In the words of the great teacher, Alan Watts, these moments helped shape me to "become who I really was." Though we all experience them, our acknowledgment of these type of profound and existential snapshots in time have become exceedingly rare.

This is because in our hyper-rationalist culture we tend to emphasize doing and acquiring over being and loving. However, learning to be and to love is exactly what we need right now if we are to transcend the suffering that this pandemic has inflicted on humanity. Becoming who we are, in an age when all our vulnerabilities are laid to bare, can feel especially daunting and heavy. But being and loving will always allow us to confront our deepest fears and anxieties with a certain quality of joy, lightness, and acceptance of what truly is. This way of relating to the world can help us all get on with our healing.

Do you find yourself consumed with worry that another pandemic may soon emerge after this one and claim your own life or that of a loved one? Just focus on staying present and genuinely show love to everyone you meet, and you will be able to embrace whatever comes your way with calm acceptance and understanding. Are you concerned that the economy might take another nosedive and leave you in desperate financial straits? Just focus on staying present and genuinely show love to everyone you meet, and you will find that no amount of financial hardship can disrupt the eternal seeds of stillness that live deep within your soul. Has all the COVID-19 related social and political unrest left you feeling afraid for the fate of humanity? Just focus on staying present and genuinely show love to everyone you meet, and you will recognize that all the current divisiveness and outrage is all passing show. One day soon, the peaceful and loving world that we all know is possible will become a reality.

When we look back on this chaotic, strange, and unsettling period in our lives the first things to be remembered will likely be external events like the shutdowns, social distancing, the economic collapse, the failed response to the pandemic by certain self-interested leaders, and the political turmoil following a divisive presidential election. However, let us also remember the way we, in the loving words of Ram Dass, used COVID-19's "fierce grace", to grow in our inner capacity to be and to love. Truly, this is the moment of our spiritual awakening. Take a deep

breath and revel in the fact that you chose a most
remarkable time to be alive!

Cheyenne Prayer for Peace

Let us know peace.

For as long as the moon shall rise,

For as long as the rivers shall flow,

For as long as the sun shall shine,

For as long as the grass shall grow,

Forrest Rivers

Appendix I: Spiritual Books to Read During a Pandemic

Be Here Now by Ram Dass

In this time of great uncertainty, the message of the late and great Baba Ram Dass, to 'be here now,' could not be more relevant. This seminal classic is many things: part spiritual biography of one saint's trippy odyssey through the layers of consciousness; part artistic work of wisdom that will break one free from dualistic thinking; and part manual for living a spiritual life. Unquestionably, *Be Here Now* was the Bible of the hippie counterculture.

The *Tao Te Ching* by Lao Tzu

Two of the positive things that have emerged from COVID-19 are the profound realization that we are all connected by some all-permeating cosmic life force (The Tao), and that rather than trying to control every event in life, we would be wise to learn how to flow with the Universe. These two realizations also happen to be two of Lao Tzu's main teachings in this mystical wisdom text.

A Year to Live by Stephen Levine

Drawing on his profound experience and work with the dying, this late and inspiring meditation teacher decided to live one year of his life as if it were his last. The result was a series of meditation exercises and profoundly rich reflections that will help one contemplate their own relationship with life and death. This book makes for a great read in a time when we all are being forced to face our own mortality.

The *Bhagavad Gita* by Krishna

Consider the power behind these words from the revered Hindu mystical text, the *Bhagavad Gita* (Song of the Lord):

"You have the right to work, but never to the fruit of work. You should never engage in action for the sake of reward, nor should you long for inaction. Perform work in this world, Arjuna, as a man established within himself—without selfish attachments, and alike in success and defeat. For yoga is perfect evenness of mind."

These words of advice from Lord Krishna, the God Incarnate, to his faithful friend and devotee, Arjuna, couldn't possibly be more relevant to the times we are currently living in. Selfless action, balance, and inner awareness are what we need right now, in our struggle against COVID-19. Lord Krishna shows us how to cultivate these inspiring qualities within ourselves.

This Season's People by Stephen Gaskin

This is a beautiful book of inspiring wisdom-oriented quotes and reflections. However, what truly adds to this book is the authenticity of its author. Stephen Gaskin was a counterculture writer and speaker, and co-founder of the Farm (one of the best-known hippie communes in the Western world) in the early '70s. As the system appears to be collapsing around us, those drawn to intentional off-the-grid spiritual communes as a peaceful alternative may find this book eye-opening.

The Dhammapada by Buddha

The First Noble Truth: Suffering is an innate characteristic of existence.

The Second Noble Truth: The cause of suffering is craving, desire, or attachment.

The Third Noble Truth: The ending of suffering can be attained by eliminating all craving, desire, or attachment.

The Fourth Noble Truth: There exists a prescribed means to end suffering (the noble Eightfold Path).

COVID-19 has produced immense physical suffering, and it is a fact of our existence at the moment (Buddha's First Noble Truth). Less obvious, to many, is that this virus has also caused enormous mental and emotional suffering. Much of this suffering can be directly attributed to our craving, desire, and attachment for existential comfort and security (Buddha's Second Noble Truth). It is heartening, though, that this suffering can be ended (Buddha's

163

Third Noble Truth) through a means-tested path to enlightenment (Buddha's Fourth Noble Truth). These core teachings of the Buddha can reveal much about our current state of being.

Ishmael by Daniel Quinn

This eco-spiritual novel centers on a telepathic gorilla-sage named Ishmael who walks a prized pupil through the unsustainability and destruction of Western civilization's relationship to the Earth. In the end, Quinn calls for something of a return to the guiding vision of indigenous cultures, whom he appropriately refers to as the 'leavers.' As our 'taker' (Quinn's name for the dominant Western culture) economy grinds to a halt, now is the perfect time to re-examine our exploitive relationship with Mother Earth and find a better way. *Ishmael* is a good place to start for exploring such solutions.

Black Elk Speaks by John G. Neihardt

Indigenous wisdom from an inspiring and highly revered Native American Medicine Man. The profound insight that he shares through his life story comes directly through ecstatic visions he had through divine communion with the Great Mystery. What could be more needed at this moment than getting back to the deep and wise roots of our native ancestors—the true spirit guardians of this land?

The Upanishads

A mind-blowing and soulfully revealing collection of mystical Hindu texts written by unknown saints and sages. Existential themes addressed that are acutely relevant to our times include the meaning of death, the nature of God, reincarnation, inner wisdom, and meditation.

Beloved honorable mentions:

The Perennial Philosophy by Aldous Huxley (Harper Collins)

The Tibetan Book of the Dead by Padmasambhava (multiple translations and publishers)

The Prophet by Kahlil Gibran (multiple translations and publishers)

Appendix II: Meditations

Mindfulness Meditation:

"Breathe in, follow your breath in through your nostrils, then into your throat, then into your lungs and belly. Sit straight, keep your eyes open but looking at the ground and with a soft focus. If you want to close your eyes, that's fine. As you breathe out, follow your breath out back into the world. If it helps, count ... one breath in, two breath out, three breath in, four breath out ... when you get to 10, start over. If you lose track, start over. If you find your mind wandering (and you will), just pay attention to your mind wandering, then bring it gently back to your breath. Repeat this process for the few minutes you meditate".

Clear Pink Light Visualization:
"Find a comfortable position---sitting in either "lotus" position on the ground or up straight in a chair. Now, slowly close your eyes and turn your mind's attention on your breath. Breathe in, breathe out. Breathe in, breathe out. Now, as you inhale, imagine breathing in

167

a clear white light. Let that light settle within your heart. Now, exhale, and picture that same white light spreading out across the room and covering each person like a blanket. Feel the radiant warmth of this light and the perfect calm that fills the room. This stillness is your essence. This stillness is your being. This stillness is presence. This still is oneness. Continue to follow your breath. Breathe the clear white light into your heart. Breathe it back out to the room. Breathe in. Breathe out. Breathe in. Breathe out. Now, after each out-breath repeat the following phrase to yourself: May all beings be peaceful, may all beings be free. Breathe in, breathe out. May all beings be peaceful, may all beings be free. Breathe in, Breathe out. Now, slowly open your eyes and sit in silence for a minute before exiting the exercise.

Walking Meditation:

Set aside a couple of hours for a slow and meditative walk through the woods. As you walk, immerse yourself in the majesty of nature and observe the stunning combination of beauty, truth, wonder, and balance in the wild. Reflect on the birth and evolution of the Earth and marvel at how her diverse features merge to form one picture-perfect mosaic. Take note of sights, sounds, and smells. Then feel as your being becomes one with the trees, rocks, soil, and sky. If your mind starts to wander, bring your attention to your breath, and repeat this mantra to yourself: "I am one with the Earth." Repeat the phrase: "I am one with the Earth." Repeat this mantra as many times as necessary. Continue to walk in silence.

About the Author

Forrest Rivers is a writer, teacher, and speaker who splits his time between the beautiful Blue Ridge mountains of North Carolina and the Colorado Rockies.

His personal journey of awakening began at the age of 30 on an awe-inspiring trip to Maui, Hawaii. It was there on that enchanted island where the profound healing power of the Earth spoke through to his heart and helped him overcome a period of alcohol abuse.

After returning home from that transformative experience, Forrest became interested in the spiritual traditions of the Far East and began to immerse himself in the teachings of Buddhist, Hindu, and Taoist mystics.

Today, Forrest spends his time guiding others to look within and become the best versions of themselves. He is author of *The Hippie Revival and Collected Writings*.

Made in the USA
Monee, IL
23 March 2021

62835911R00105